Kant's *Critique of Pui*

In Memoriam

Judith Helen Beale
(1947–2004)

Kant's *Critique of Pure Reason*

An Orientation to the Central Theme

Anthony Savile

Blackwell
Publishing

BLACKWELL PUBLISHING
350 Main Street, Malden, MA 02148-5020, USA
9600 Garsington Road, Oxford OX4 2DQ, UK
550 Swanston Street, Carlton, Victoria 3053, Australia

First published 2005 by Blackwell Publishing Ltd

1 2005

Library of Congress Cataloging-in-Publication Data

Savile, Anthony.
    Kant's Critique of pure reason : an orientation to the central theme / Anthony Savile.
        p. cm.
    Includes bibliographical references and index.
    ISBN 1-4051-2040-1 (alk. paper) – ISBN 1-4051-2041-X (pbk. : alk. paper)
        1. Kant, Immanuel, 1724–1804. Kritik der reinen Vernunft. I. Title.

B2779.S28 2005
121–dc22

2004019909

ISBN–13: 978-1-4051-2040-1 (alk. paper)
ISBN–13: 978-1-4051-2041-8 (pbk. :alk. paper)

A catalogue record for this title is available from the British Library.

Set in 10 on 12pt Sabon
by Kolam Information Services Pvt. Ltd, Pondicherry, India
Printed and bound in the United Kingdom
by TJ International, Padstow, Cornwall

The publisher's policy is to use permanent paper from mills that operate a sustainable forestry policy, and which has been manufactured from pulp processed using acid-free and elementary chlorine-free practices. Furthermore, the publisher ensures that the text paper and cover board used have met acceptable environmental accreditation standards.

For further information on
Blackwell Publishing, visit our website:
www.blackwellpublishing.com

Contents

1
Historical Prelude

'Above all, my truth-seeking young friends, beware of letting our professors tell you what is contained in the *Critique of Pure Reason*.'

–Schopenhauer

Immanuel Kant's *Critique of Pure Reason*, first published in 1781, is one of the glories of modern Western philosophy. Its title declares its overall theme. That is the question of what knowledge we can acquire through the exercise of reason alone, independently of all sensory experience. The broad answer Kant proposes is that while reason can teach us much about the nature and structure of our cognitive grasp of the world, it cannot itself deliver any determinate matter of substance. That is the business of experience, not ratiocination, and the traditional pretensions of reason to supplement, or stand in for, experience here under the title of speculative metaphysics are revealed as entirely illusory.

This response to the central question determines the structure of the whole work. Broadly speaking, its first half is devoted to the positive aspect of the answer, where Kant sets out his famous doctrine of Transcendental Idealism. That doctrine, which is, indeed, held in place by reason alone, proposes to show how sensible experience is competent to furnish knowledge of the world, and to do so in a way that is immune to the various difficulties with that seemingly truistic thought which had beset Kant's immediate predecessors. The second, more negative, half of the *Critique* focuses on what Kant sees as the failures of traditional metaphysics, which had aimed, through the power of reason alone, to attain insights about the world more secure than any that mere experience might provide. There Kant is concerned to identify the limits that reason should set to its own ambitions, and to demonstrate how earlier and contemporary philosophy had ridden roughshod over them. In these pages I set that large portion of the *Critique* aside and concern myself exclusively with the positive account of knowledge-enabling experience that Kant develops in his work's earlier parts.

Putting it for the moment very roughly, Kant's principal teaching is that the world experience reveals to us, and about which we can attain reputable empirical knowledge, is in large part constituted by ourselves and our own ways of thought. It is a world that we must understand to be coloured through and through by the nature of our own minds. For this reason, if for no other, it is to be thought of as *the world as it appears* and not as *the world as it is in itself*. By contrast, Kant's predecessors had usually taken the world we aspire to know and understand as having its character fixed quite independently of the mental capacities that we bring to bear upon it. For them, knowledge of the world was absolute knowledge, knowledge of the world as it is in itself. We shall need to appreciate the enormous difficulties that Kant believed this natural, and largely unquestioned, assumption encountered if we are to understand what he proposed to put in its place. For him, the rather negative doctrine of Transcendental Idealism was not just as a way of avoiding those difficulties; besides that, and together with its more positive dual, Empirical Realism, it aimed to articulate a more stable view of the relation that must hold between creatures with minds like ours and any world that is cognitively accessible to them.

To understand how Kant arrived at this striking position and to appreciate its many merits we need to be clear about the historical setting from which it laboriously emerged. The point of departure here lies with the work of René Descartes, whose *Meditations on First Philosophy* had been composed a century and a half or so before Kant embarked on the *Critique*. Struggling to explain our right to claim far-reaching knowledge of the world and, more particularly, to account for our prospects for making sound scientific sense of it, Descartes had taught that we should only succeed to the extent that our world-oriented beliefs could be rendered proof against all doubt. In this way everyday knowledge of the world around us (*cognitio*) and any more taxing scientific under- standing of it we might hope to reach (*scientia*) both demanded certainty. Now, evidently, both our everyday beliefs about the world and our more theoretically driven scientific ones are, at the end of the day, largely rooted in one form or another of sensory perception, as, for example, are my beliefs that snow has fallen during the night, that the trains are none the less running on time, and even such highly theoretical matters as that $e = mc^2$. Yet, if we take the perceptions that underpin such beliefs to be directly of the snow in the street or of the information legible on the arrivals board in the station or perhaps the trains themselves, the cer- tainties Descartes teaches us to look for seem to be lost. Possibilities of misidentification, delusion, hallucination, illusion and other sorts of error abound, and so seemed to Descartes to rule out any such worldly starting point. Instead, he had proposed that we set out from the error- proof data of our own consciousness, that is, from the certainty of how things subjectively seem to us, as opposed to how we take them objectively to be in fact. (See here in particular the *Second Meditation*.) On that unimpeachable basis, Descartes supposed that we should be able to construct secure lines of inference to the distant causes in the world beyond the mind of the mind's own stream of indubitable data. In the case of our examples, such inferences, executed with all due care, could be supposed to take us faultlessly to the presence of snow in the street and to the existence of information posted on the arrivals board, and thence, further down the line, to impeccable knowledge that snow has fallen in the night, and that, even so, the trains are running on time. Similarly, too, though undoubtedly in more complex fashion, with the sort of knowledge that we take it to be the business of the natural sciences ultimately to provide, such as knowledge about the fundamental nature of energy and of light.

Descartes' choice of starting point was heavy with consequence for the century that followed, since his principal successors, both on the continent of Europe as well as in off-shore Britain, all assumed that Descartes' privileging of the mind's own indubitable subjective contents could not be gainsaid. The trouble, it quickly came to be seen, came with knowing how to proceed from there. The alternatives that were canvassed and which engaged Kant at the end of the eighteenth century are swiftly enough set out.

First, there is Descartes' own strategy. We set out from certainties about the mind's own present contents, and then, drawing to the very best of our ability on our God-given resources of sense, memory and understanding, we infer to the nature of the distant causes of those subjective states (cf. *Sixth Meditation, ad finem*). Exercising our intellect with all possible care, we exclude all grounds of doubt that might beset us, and once that is done – and just to the extent it can be done – we are to trust God benevolently to ensure that the beliefs we form by way of the best explanation of those close-to-home indubitable subjective effects are indeed true ones. In this way Descartes held our possession of perceptually based knowledge about the world around us to be secure. Analogous reflection was presumed to support the more ambitious aspirations of the natural sciences to provide us with systematic insight into the world's workings.

Next, on the English side of the Channel, and at the end of the seventeenth century, we find John Locke endorsing the broad lines of Descartes' epistemology, only with the important difference that for him appeal to God and His benevolence have in all consistency to be treated as somewhat insecure empirical matters, on a par with other beliefs about the world beyond the mind.[1] So, the all-important theological props on which Descartes had relied to secure certainty for the inferences that were to yield knowledge of the surrounding world beyond the mind were simply not available. The upshot for Locke was that our speculations about the causes of our subjective mental states enjoy at best probability, not certainty, and both we and the practising scientist have to content ourselves with that. Whereas Descartes proudly claimed to possess a route to knowledge of the world beyond the mind, Locke more modestly acknowledges our extensive and unavoidable ignorance of it. The most we can know is that there exists beyond the mind some present cause of our various 'ideas' and that it must be varied enough in its nature to account for the variety of impressions that are registered by our senses (cf. *An Essay concerning Human Understanding*, IV.xi.2).

Writing in the wake of Locke, the Irish divine, George Berkeley, was convinced that the subjective starting point that Locke and Descartes had both assumed was unassailable. He was, however, insistent that inference could not play the fundamental role that those two thinkers had assigned to it in accounting for either certain or probable insight about the world. Seeing their over-optimistic inferential procedures as opening the way to an intolerable scepticism – eventually, even to atheism – Berkeley sought to cut the knot by the drastic expedient of identifying the natural world itself with those very mental states, otherwise known as 'ideas', whose character we could not doubt. Much knowledge of the kind we unhesitatingly claim about the world could then be taken as given to us directly in our having those very mental states, and then there would no need to appeal to dubious inferences to account for its possession.

Lastly, for Kant's closer contemporary, David Hume, Berkeley's radical solution to the problem facing him was, like that of his predecessors, quite uncompelling. Even though perception is, indeed, immediately of our sensory impressions, or Berkeleyan ideas, the worldly objects of common sense and scientific investigation are, as we conceive of them, independent of us. Hence they must be distinct from our mental states and cannot be identical with them. Moreover, we think of them as persisting through breaks in the flow of our conscious states, which Berkeley's proposal could scarcely consistently acknowledge. However, Hume thought he could show that it lies quite beyond our power to prove that such things do actually exist. Our various faculties of mind, reason, sense and imagination are all impotent in that regard. In consequence, we should abandon the old Cartesian quest for secure knowledge and simply accept that we have an inbuilt natural propensity to believe in the existence of the extra-mental world, a propensity that we are quite incapable of shaking off in the conduct of our everyday life. In the quiet of the study, it is true, we cannot avoid out-and-out scepticism (as Berkeley himself had feared in his reflections on Locke), but once outside its doors and going about our daily business, we find the natural world's unamenability to philosophical proof has no hold over us. The acceptance of philosophical scepticism has no implications for life itself.

Kant's view of these various responses to the original problem was unremittingly hostile. From his point of view, they are as quickly dismissed as they are set out. Descartes' approach suffered on two counts. It relied on invalid argument in establishing the existence of a benevolent God; and then, its pretension to erect compelling and indubitable hypotheses about the distal causes of our immediately given sensory states was overblown. Once we set aside the theology, the fact that we can find no better explanation for the perceptual states we enjoy than the existence of a world of mind-independent objects that cause those states may perhaps account for our *feeling* certain about their existence, but that can scarcely make their *existence* certain. Yet, in the matter of knowledge, be that demanding *scientia* or mere everyday *cognitio*, it is the latter certainty that is at issue, not the former. As Kant would see it, speculative inferences erected on such a narrow base could not even lay claim to the sort of probability that Locke was optimistically prepared to accord them, let alone certainty of the kind required by Descartes. Such views should be dismissed as little more than pious 'enthusiasm' (B128).[2]

Berkeley's alternative way of making the distant, extra-mental, world accessible to us, namely by depriving it of its very distance, fares no better. The outright identification of the world of common sense with our sensations, or 'ideas', signally failed to preserve the crucial distinction between reality and illusion, and that Kant insisted was far too high a price to pay. No acceptable philosophy can secure our knowledge of the world at the cost of 'degrading bodies to mere illusion' as he puts it at B71. Finally, Hume's urbane form of scepticism leaves us in the scandalous position of abandoning all serious claim to know that we live in the world at all (Bxxxix fn.). Just being natively unable to resist the belief that we do so is no consolation to philosophy, which can hardly earn its spurs by blithely renouncing the task of providing intellectual support for our very most basic beliefs.

While epistemological concern for the world beyond the mind provided one notable stimulus to the *Critique*, Kant's manner of proceeding was also responsive to other, for him deeper, inherited philosophical problems. Two of these demand to be noticed at the outset. The first is that of explaining the very ability we have even so much as to *think* about a world that is distinct from us, whether or not such thought terminates in knowledge. Thinking about the world is of course an ability we exercise even as we ask how our belief in the existence of such a thing can be justified. For Descartes, it passed without question that the indubitable data of sensation already came replete with that extra-mental content. After all, whether I am right to think so or not, it is now to me subjectively *as if* I am confronted by the façade of a house illuminated by the brightly shining sun; it is now to me *as if* the trains are running on time, and so on. However, given that by Descartes' own reckoning our senses do not themselves *immediately* acquaint us with such things as houses and their façades, the shining sun or the punctual trains,[3] and that we allegedly know about such things only through the construction of inferences from the sensory data that are immediately given to us, the question presses whence it comes that we are equipped with the conceptual stock we need to possess if we are to fashion those inferences and formulate their conclusions. The answer evidently cannot rightly be provided by the purely phenomenal character of our sensory experience. Nor can it be given by appeal to imagination (which, for Descartes and Locke, can do no more than put together simple elements that our mental experience itself provides). So it seems that, for Descartes at least, we have to turn to God again to supply us benevolently with such concepts innately.[4] From Kant's point of view that is to do no better than to explain one mystery by another, an even darker one.

Locke at least was not drawn in that particular direction. Rejecting all appeal to the innateness of our cognitive stock as theoretically otiose, in his *Essay* (1690) he had attempted to account for our ability to entertain thought about external bodies as fully explicable in terms of our capacity to combine elementary ideas, directly given in sensation. Laudable though the attempt may have been, it was none the less doomed from the start. As we have already seen Hume pointing out, the fundamental conception we have of the physical world involves the idea that it exists in independence of ourselves and of our minds. Yet nothing that is directly given to the mind by way of bare sensation, as Locke had conceived of it, has that solid character about it; nor can our simple ideas, whose content merely captures the phenomenal quality of those sensations themselves, be combined to generate that demanding idea of independence; so, once again, our very ability to think in such terms returns as acutely problematic. And if that is problematic, how much more so must be the ability Locke presumed we enjoy to construct probable inferences to the supposedly distant causes of our sensory experience. Such inferences have to be expressed in terms whose content extends far beyond anything ascribable to the data from which they set out, and, eschewing Cartesian nativism, Locke's empirical alternative has no clear way of making good the deficiency. That is a second problem from which Kant sets out, the solution to which dominates his whole philosophy of experience.

The remaining topic to bear in mind at the outset, distinct from, though closely related to, those just discussed, concerns the issue of causality. The world in which we live and which we think of ourselves as exploring through our experience is not just a collection of disparate individuals unrelated to one another; it consists of things that have their effects on us and which stand in complex causal relations to one another. Descartes' advocacy of mechanistic ways of thinking about the world and the advance of the physical sciences in the seventeenth century made such thought philosophically commonplace and theoretically quite irreversible. Analytical metaphysics, however, had not kept pace with this theoretical advance. It seemed evident to Kant that to recognize causality in the world is possible only if some necessity can be discerned that relates causes and their effects, yet the resources of established philosophy were quite inadequate to the task since such necessity would, it seemed, have to be viewed either as purely logical matter – which would clearly not be to the point – or, alternatively, to be reduced to a species of empirical regularity – patently too weak to do the job (A91–2/B124). So, theoretically speaking, not knowing what we should be looking for, contemporary epistemology was impotent to justify the claims about the world we cast in causal terms, thus rendering some of our most fundamental beliefs about it nugatory, even when taken in abstraction from the other difficulties raised so far.

Then, just as with our concept of material things, it was hard to account for our possession of any respectable *concept* of causation anyway. Appeal to the God-given innateness of such an idea was unacceptably *ad hoc*, yet accounting for it empirically failed to supply any grasp of the necessity internal to the causal relation from anything given to experience taken in the narrow subjective way that seemed natural to Locke and his successors. So, as Kant surveyed the intellectual landscape before him, not only did systematic causal knowledge of the natural world that presents itself to us in everyday thought seem to lie beyond our reach; in addition, we appeared not to have even the first clue about how it is possible for us to *think* of our world in such terms. Yet since the natural world is precisely a domain of law and causality, our very ability to conceive of ourselves as part of the natural order was under threat, or at the very least hung precariously in the air.

With Transcendental Idealism Kant took himself to have a compelling resolution to these problems. In the following chapters I set out the structure of his reasoning in some detail, but it will be useful to sketch its broad outline now in a preliminary way while setting aside all question of its internal justification. To do this here will at least make it plain why Kant should have proudly talked of his philosophy as engineering a

Copernican revolution in the subject, and also make plain why he had no little reason for pride.

First of all, we see Kant abandoning the central assumption that guided the various thinkers just mentioned to the effect that what we are immediately aware of in perception are our own conscious sensory states of mind, the buzzing array of indubitable sensation that we find it so difficult to describe except in terms of what we take to be its causes. We do indeed enjoy such arrays – the 'manifold of intuition' as Kant calls them – but what is immediately given to us in our experience of things are not those manifolds themselves, but *appearances*, by which Kant quite generally means things in the world as they present themselves to us. My experience presents the world to me in the guise of a punctual train or the shining sun or the façade of a house, and I do not have to devise some far-fetched inferential story to explain how I come to be aware of these things. In favourable circumstances, they are immediately given to me in the experience that is mine and which I have formed ('synthesized', in Kant's vocabulary) in making sense of that initially unconceptualized sensory array, that 'manifold'.[5]

As I have just expressed it, there is bound to be uncertainty whether the appearances with which Kant holds experience to acquaint us are anything other than the interpretations we put upon the sensations or sensory input that his predecessors thought we had to start out from, or whether they are to be understood as objects in the world beyond the mind and which we are acquainted with in perception. If they are the former, as Kant's talk of appearances as 'syntheses of the manifold of intuition' might suggest, it must look as if he is hardly distancing himself from the subjective and Cartesianly inspired starting point of his predecessors. After all, it seems uncontroversial that we interpret the content of our perceptual input in terms of what we take to occasion it, but the philosophical question of our intellectual right to do that is what is at issue. On this view of what Kant means by 'appearance', that question looks untouched, and the accuracy of our interpretations to the world itself remains quite inscrutable. On the other hand, if 'appearances' are taken in the second, somewhat Pickwickian, way, as designating objects in the world, Kant is likely to be seen as just dogmatically sweeping the original epistemological problem under the carpet, and not advancing its solution one whit. Does not the old question remain: With what right can we say that our perceptual experience is ever of objects beyond our experience itself? How can the answer to that question be advanced by calling such things 'appearances'?

It would be Kant's view that this puzzlement should evaporate as the precise nature of his position becomes clear. The pressure to start from bare, sensory content originated with a preoccupation with certainty. And that, Kant sees, rests on a mistake. The certainty that is provided by our perceptual states depends on their relation to other beliefs that we have, not on our finding some minimally exposed characterization of the data from which we start. When perceptual experience furnishes us with knowledge – which is what we suppose it generally provides – we make sense of our perceptual input ('combine or synthesize the manifold of intuition') in ways that, in the light of other beliefs we have, are liable to resist further revision. In favourable circumstances we then have certainty enough. The fact that in other situations we might synthesize the manifold in the same way, only erroneously so rather than accurately, does nothing at all to suggest that when things are working well our judgements do not enjoy secure support (B278–9). The move to worldly appearance, and away from would-be rock solid indubitable sensory data, does nothing to abandon what is legitimate about the demand for certainty. It does, however, adjust somewhat the way we understand it, and, Kant would say, adjust it for the better.

As for the issue of truth and accuracy, while you or I can clearly have experience as of a punctual train when the wretched thing is well overdue, that does nothing at all to show (and Descartes notwithstanding – see note 3) that there are not also situations, standard ones indeed, in which when our perception is as of the train's punctuality, what appears to us is just that, a punctual train. In circumstances of that kind, Kant will say we are not making any inference of the sort that seemed to his predecessors to be inevitable. The truth of the matter is given to us in our perception itself, and when it is, and our grounds for believing it are grounds that resist revision, then our perceptual experience supplies us directly with knowledge of the world beyond.

Putting it a little more fully, particular perceptual episodes may present us with any of these three situations:

a) It is to me as if I am presented with something that is F (for instance, a train that is on time), and that is a mistake (the train is in fact overdue)

b) It is to me as if I am presented with something that is F, and an F thing is just what is present to me, where the reason for its being to me as if I am presented with something that is F is nothing other than that that is what is present to me. (I take myself to see a punctual train, and do so just because that is what is before my eyes.)

c) As with (b), but with the difference that something other than the presence of an F thing accounts for its seeming to me that that is what is present (perhaps I have been primed by over-enthusiastic railway staff to expect to see a punctual train, and so take the train before me to be on time, and as it happens, and quite surprisingly, that is exactly what it is).

The first and last of these three are clearly epistemically off-colour, and the second is the state in which we standardly aim to be. Now, in answer to the question posed, Kant can say that in that latter case, the experience we have (the outcome of the synthesis of the manifold we, generally unhesitatingly, come to) can be described *both* in terms of the interpretation we place on the buzzing array of data given to us on an occasion, and *also* in terms of what it is that so appears to us, the punctual train or the brightly coloured house façade, or whatever else it may be. Any duality in the use of the term 'appearance' merely reflects the nature of veridical experience, experience in which what is the case presents itself to us as just that, what it is.[6]

Nothing in what I have yet said seems suggestive of any Copernican revolution; indeed, nothing said will sound particularly 'Kantian', and nothing said pretends to explain just why Kant talks of the world open to experience as a world of appearances in the fullest sense he gave that term, and which has not yet been properly brought out. None the less, as far as it goes, it is accurate to his thought, and putting it as I have done usefully prepares us for the revolutionary step that is to come. That step passes through the concern raised above about the puzzling origin of the conceptual stock on which we rely in synthesizing the data that we passively receive from the world itself. In particular, it relies on many features that could not be extracted from the narrowly conceived sources of experience, the manifold, on which, with varying degrees of insouciance, Kant's forerunners allowed themselves to draw.

For the sake of immediate illustration, and just because I have already insisted on its importance above, let us focus on the case of causation. As we articulate our experience, we often say we are aware of things in causal terms. We feel the sun ripening the tomatoes; we hear the hammer crack the nut; we watch a friend succumb to the illness that ails him, and so on. And we think that there is no reason why such matters as these should not fit into pattern (b) above, where the crucial causal terms have their place in our synthesizing of the manifold and also in the world that, at its best, truth-oriented synthesizing reveals to us.

As Kant views it, just because the idea of causality that is drawn on in such judgements involves the notion of necessary connection (between cause and effect), the world as it is in itself cannot possibly encompass any such thing. And because it cannot do that, we cannot look to the world in itself as the explanatory source for that particular item of our conceptual repertoire. We cannot have acquired the concept *cause* from experiential encounters with the world no matter how rich those encounters may have been; hence we need a different way of accounting for our possession of it. On the other hand, we have no compelling reason to suppose, in good Cartesian fashion, that we are fortuitously presented with that idea and its like as from the hand of God, a beneficent gift without which we would not be able to discern how the world that He created is constituted, for in this particular case necessary connections do not lie in the world at all, and any God-given innate idea that intimated to us that they did could only misrepresent it (B167–8). Rather, and this is the point at which we at last come upon Kant's revolutionary step, the idea of causation is one we are bound to use just because it is an expression of our mind's own constitution. So too with other fundamental concepts such as those of space and time and their many derivatives[7] that we shall meet as we progress. Here lies the source of Kant's insistence that the world we experience is the world *as it appears*, rather than the world as it is in itself.

The mind we bring to the world is, for Kant, well thought of in terms of the functions it performs. In particular, we should understand it in terms of the way in which in our experience, via the operation of the understanding, the mind functions to bring the sensibly given manifold under concepts. In doing this, Kant thinks, one of the central concepts the mind is of its own nature obliged to employ is that of causation. The result is that the world the mind reveals to us experiences is one in which causal relations are seen as, indeed are directly experienced as, holding.

Does that mean then that we misperceive the world? After all, if the world on its own account, and thought of as existing entirely independently of us, contains no necessary connections, and yet we are obliged by our own nature to experience it in such terms, it will seem that we are bound to misinterpret the world and thereby precisely *fail* to have knowledge of it in just those cases in which we think we grasp it best. Here we come to the second stage of the Kantian revolution: for not only are we obliged to view the world through the focus of our own intellectual make up by using concepts that have their roots in our own constitution, but we have to see that the world that reveals itself to us, the world of appearance, is itself partially constituted by the way in which our minds capture it. That, thinks Kant, rightly or wrongly, is the way to avoid the conclusion that we are bound to misrepresent it. As long as we restrict ourselves to investigation of world as it appears, our experience is generally accurate enough. When things go well, we do not systematically misrepresent that. Misrepresentation would only dog us if we thought to have experience of the world as it is in itself and on its own account. Once we forswear that unrealizable ambition, all significant sceptical worries can be met.

The world that appears, then, is the world as it truly is, and it emphatically contrasts with any view of the world as *mere* appearance. Kant is clear in his own mind about that (B69–70). For him, appearances present features of the world to us that can only be captured by creatures with our sort of intellectual resources, features that cannot be attributed to the world except in relation to ourselves, and which cannot be thought to characterize it as it is on its own account in complete independence of us. For this reason, specifically with regard to questions of causality, but, as we shall see, with other fundamental concepts too, we can indeed say that the nature of the world reveals itself to us *truly* in our experience. However, when it does so, what is revealed to us is the world of appearance only, not the world as it is in itself, where the word 'appearance' now carries with it the further, peculiarly Kantian, implication that what we experience is in part a reflection of ourselves. On occasion Kant does indeed suggest, hyperbolically, that to this extent the world is of the mind's own making (A42/B60, A114, A370), but that is something of an exaggeration: more modestly put, his position is that the world reveals itself to us as possessing features that can only be understood in terms of our particular way of grasping it. To recognize this and to see just how extensively that thought reaches is to appreciate that there are significant limits to the experiential knowledge we can have of the world, but since the preoccupations of earlier thinkers were confined to what lies within those limits anyway, and did not touch the question of mapping those borders, the problems with which they had struggled are ones which are, as Kant saw it, effectively resolved. Transcendental Idealism, understood now as the doctrine that we cannot know the world as it is in itself, but that we do have direct experiential access to the world of appearance was the final, hitherto overlooked, alternative to those that Kant's predecessors had canvassed in their epistemological endeavours.[8] Where they had all failed, Kant believed himself at last to have met with success.

So much for an outline of Kant's response to his main precursors. In sum: we do not have knowledge of the world by inference from our narrowly conceived 'bare' experience. Rather, we experience the world, amply given, directly, and when things go well we experience it with all the certainty that can reasonably be required. Then, while much of our conceptual stock is acquired from the world that we encounter, there are a number of fundamental concepts, of which I have so far mentioned only *causation*, but which include the concepts *space* and *time* and all their many determinations, which we cannot come by in that fashion. Instead, they are concepts which we are obliged to deploy in the exercise of those very intellectual functions that define the mind itself. A consequence of this is that the world that reveals itself to us in appearance has to be thought of as peculiarly ours, or as a world of our own fashioning. That is Kant's would-be Copernican revolution. The insight that our understanding of the world has to conform to that revolution is, for Kant, the primordial example of the sort of knowledge that pure reason can provide. There are, of course, more and less palatable ways of taking this idea. In this preliminary, often rather loose, exposition of the *Critique*'s main theme I have aimed to present it in a way that is as little estranging as possible. The extent to which it is a view that can be sustained either as a tenable interpretation of Kant's own text or as sound philosophy in its own right will be something to test as we move on and turn this somewhat rough and ready initial sketch into something more precisely and carefully worked.

2

Sensibility, Space and Time

To announce a revolution in philosophy is one thing; to accomplish it, another. Kant proposes to do so by close examination of the contributions made to experience by sensibility and by understanding, those two faculties of mind that are engaged whenever we take either outer perception or inner reflection to reveal something of the world to us, be that externally, about things distinct from ourselves, or internally, about our own mental lives. The first of these is treated in the relatively short passage of the *Critique* entitled 'Transcendental Aesthetic', and it is that which concerns us now.

The title of this part of Kant's book is informative enough. Although the term 'aesthetic' might suggest concern with beauty and its cognates, he makes plain that that is not what he has in mind (A21/B35 fn.). His usage merely draws on the etymology of the Greek word 'aisthesis', meaning *sensation*, or *perception*, and what is discussed in the Aesthetic is simply the contribution made to experience by sensibility, that element of experience in which we are passive recipients of sensory stimuli. As for 'transcendental', that is a term that had a reputable technical use in earlier philosophy, but to which Kant came to give a novel twist. In his vocabulary, *transcendental* matters are such as are concerned with those conditions that have to be satisfied by something for it to be possible.[1] So, what the Transcendental Aesthetic is concerned with are those absolutely general conditions that must be satisfied if our experience is to be *sensory* experience at all, conditions on the possibility of our having any sense-based experience whatsoever.

Obviously enough, a great deal of the sensory information we have about the world just depends on how the world happens to be. With that Kant would not disagree. But it is his firm conviction that, in addition to that, there are quite general and purely formal constraints on what sensibility can reveal to us. These 'transcendental' constraints do not depend in the least on what the world is in fact like; instead, they reflect the nature of sensibility itself, and depend on the structure of any minds, human or not, that are reliant on sensibility in fashioning the experience that its possessors come to have.

The principal thesis that Kant is concerned to establish here is that, surprising as it may seem, the very spatio-temporal character of our world has to be understood in that transcendental and formal way. Correspondingly, its pervasiveness throughout experience is ascribable not to the nature of world itself but to our fundamental dependence on sensibility for experiencing it. Because it is an *a priori* matter that sensible experience cannot detach itself from these conditions of spatiality and temporality, Kant takes it that we can say, once again as a matter of pure reason, that any world which we, or other creatures dependent on our sort of sensibility, might come to experience is bound to reveal itself through the very same spatio-temporal structure as informs the world that is actually ours. Here is the first major strut in the positive metaphysic that Kant aims to establish.

While Kant thinks of the transcendental elements of experience as its *form*, by contrast, he regards its variable and contingent content, supplied from the side of the world revealed to us in perception, as its *matter*. So, this first substantial portion of the *Critique* has in its sights an investigation of those formal, non-contingent elements of experience that our dependence on sensibility prescribes to it and which set determinate limits to what the world of our experience could materially be like. In a later chapter we shall see the next major section of Kant's book, the Transcendental Analytic, mounting an analogous enquiry in respect of the other essential faculty of mind involved in the constitution of experience, understanding. There, too, the investigation is concerned with the question of form rather than of matter, and there, as here, we find in this form/matter distinction the roots of Kant's particular kind of idealism, which at bottom amounts to the doctrine that such experience as we have can only be of a world that is formally shaped by the faculties of mind that we exercise in attaining it. All this, however, is as yet entirely programmatic. We want to know what arguments move Kant to pursue this unprecedented programme.

Any experience I have of my own inner states takes place in time; any experience I have of things other than my conscious self will involve locating them in space. These are observations which Kant's predecessors would have found truistic and uncontestable. Setting out from here, however, Kant soon goes on in ways that would have met with protest. To have experience of things *as* spatial and *as* temporal, *as* situated in space and time, we have to possess the concepts *space* and *time*, and for those concepts to enjoy the *bona fides* that they are assumed by all parties to have there needs to be an acceptable account of their origin, an account of how we come to possess them. So far, so good. Kant's empiricist predecessors, most notably John Locke, had taught that those concepts, like any others, have their roots in experience itself (cf. *Essay*, II.xiii and xiv). We encounter things and events that stand in spatial and temporal relations to one another, things that enjoy spatial and temporal location, dimension and so forth, and, noticing the recurrence of such things in perception and by abstracting from their individual particularities, we come to fashion appropriate general concepts that permit us to think quite freely in such terms. Thus the concepts *space* and *time*, just like any others, are empirically acquired – so Locke had taught – and once acquired are ready to be deployed in articulating our view of the world around us, ultimately just because that is the way the world happens to be. Putting it rather strangely, but entirely in line with Locke's overall teaching, if the world that had presented itself to our senses had been very different, then maybe it wouldn't have presented itself to us as a spatio-temporal world at all. Then, of course, we should not have had a use for those concepts, if we could so much as even form them. That we do think in spatio-temporal terms is basically a reflection of the world that happens to be ours, not of any particular psychological, physiological or biological dependence on sensibility for experiencing it.

To Kant's way of thinking, this seemingly harmless line of reasoning was utterly misconceived. It just could not be the case that the concepts *space* and *time* should be acquired like that. They have to be accounted for in some other way, and the only viable possibility that he sees is that they are given to us just in virtue of our being creatures whose access to the world is mediated by the mind's dependence on sensibility. Spatiality and temporality are the *forms* of sensible experience itself, and the mistake that Locke and his followers were making was to confuse that with the contingent *matter* of experience, for which alone the Lockean account of abstractive concept-formation can hold good. This is what lies at the heart of Kant's rejection of classical empiricism, and the conclusion is not just arrived at dogmatically; it has the support of a typically condensed and frustratingly obscure argument.

What is to be shown is that '*space* is not an empirical concept which has been derived from outer experiences'. Kant proceeds: 'For in order that certain sensations be referred to something outside me (that is, to something in another region of space from that in which I find myself), and similarly in order that I may be able to represent them as outside and alongside one another, and accordingly as not only different but as in different places, the representation of space must be presupposed'

(A23/B38). The leading idea here appears simple enough. We could not acquire these concepts from experience, because any attempt to do so would have to assume that we already possessed them, and so the attempt fails. The difficulty is to see exactly how this argument is meant to work.

It is natural enough to view it as an assault on a particular application of Locke's abstractionist conception of concept-formation, which is just what many commentators do. Seeing it like that, we are to reflect that in order to come by the concepts *space*, or *spatiality*, and *time*, or *temporality*, we would need to conceive of the individuals and events on the basis of which we learn those ideas as of more or less precisely located space/time-occupiers, and so already effectively possess the concepts whose origin we are trying to explain. Hence we couldn't acquire such concepts empirically unless we already possessed them, in which case we couldn't acquire them empirically at all. The trouble is that if Kant's argument is no better than this it must be judged particularly lame, since it does nothing to rule out the possibility that the concepts *space* and *place*, or *location*, should be acquired together rather than sequentially. In addition, it leaves it quite obscure how genuinely empirical concepts could be empirically learnt. So, for example, in order to come by the concept *grey* abstractively, must I not do so by way of first seeing individuals *as* grey? And does that not likewise presuppose that the concept *grey* is already possessed if I am to look to experience to account for its acquisition?

These points, however, may bear less on Kant than on his commentators, since in the very next paragraphs Kant insists that [the concept] *space* is not a general concept at all, and so it is entirely reasonable to suppose that any arguments against its being an empirically learnt *general* concept would just miss the target. What is wanted is a reading of his thought that counts against the concept *space* being learnt empirically whether it be a singular or a general one (something about which Kant is for the moment silent). Furthermore, as the query about the concept *grey* shows, the argument Kant is using needs to be one that leaves ample room for concepts that are undoubtedly empirical, truly dependent on the sort of material experience that comes our way. Without something that looks better able to meet these demands, he will not have what he wants, and the initial foundation stone of his transcendental idealism will fail to support the ambitious superstructure that comes to rest upon it.

Fortunately, as long as we keep in mind the historical perspective from which Kant was setting out and within the framework of which he operates, something that may serve him here is not far to seek. To the empiricist way of thinking, the very simplest concepts we have are learnt directly from the elementary flow of perceptual stimulation. It is from this that we get those primary ideas that Locke lists as of 'yellow, white, heat, cold, soft, hard, bitter, sweet, and all those which we call sensible qualities' (*Essay*, II.i.3). I have said in the last chapter that in Kant's vocabulary that simple flow of stimulation is what he calls 'the manifold of intuition', and it is entirely plausible to think that as far as genuinely empirical concepts go, like those on Locke's list, Kant would wholeheartedly agree with Locke about our route to them.[2] What is notable, though, is that if we consider our ideas of spatial and temporal extent, those ideas encounter no proper match within that elementary sensory flow when that is consciously and narrowly described. That fact alone would make it impossible for Kant to accept Locke's own story at *Essay*, II.xiii and xiv about how we come to construct the concepts *space* and *time* empirically from the repetition of simple ideas of *distance* and *duration*. Within the manifold of intuition there just are no such empirically given simple ideas.

Our sensory flow is, of course, given to us in time, but strictly speaking its temporal dimension is not itself any part of its experienced content, not an element of the manifold of intuition itself. So too with spatiality. So, as Kant puts it, if I am to 'refer certain sensations to something outside me... the representation [meaning here the *concept* – A.S.] of space must be presupposed'. In other words, we can only make use of spatial and temporal ideas in our articulation of experience providing that they *already* have a non-empirical source in the mind, external to the content of the manifold of intuition. They have to be, as Kant puts it, *a priori* representations, not empirical ones.[3] As developed in the Aesthetic (and in analogous remarks about the *a priori* concepts of the understanding discussed in the Analytic), this is the thought that lies at the heart of Kant's idealism. Once it is clearly understood, much else that seems puzzling will readily fall into place.

However it is understood, Kant's argument about the non-empirical nature of our spatio-temporal concepts can strike one as unremarkable for two separate reasons. The first is that it is entirely negative, it merely tells us what these concepts are not. Yet it is what we are obliged to think they are, the positive account of them that Kant goes on to give, that brings the surprise with it and initiates his proudly proclaimed revolution. Then, secondly, even if we were immediately convinced that we had here come across certain concepts whose origin we could not account for empirically, that of itself might seem of minor importance. Is not our empirical cognitive stock impressively rich anyway, quite independent of the contents of the non-empirical *a priori* showcase?

As for the first reflection, it is only because Kant is so sure of the negative claim that he pushes on to the positive alternative that follows.

So, if, at the end of the day, the critic wants to resist Kant's revolutionary proposals, he will have to undo what Kant offers him at this preliminary stage. He cannot simply pass over the argument in silence. As for the second, minimizing, reflection, Kant himself swiftly moves to block that. Not only is *space* an *a priori* representation, it is a *necessary a priori* representation, 'necessary' in the sense that it is one we cannot bypass. The reason is that as long as we acknowledge our dependence on sensibility, any experience that we come to have must situate its contents in space and in time. This isn't the (presumably false) thought that we cannot coherently think of space or time as empty, since as Kant makes plain (A24/B38–9) there is no contradiction in conceiving of such a thing, even if we could never experience it; rather, it is that no determinate sensible experience of something distinct from ourselves could be other than of something having its place in space and in time.[4]

While Kant offers no particular support for this intuitively plausible assertion, one which would scarcely have startled his own contemporaries, it must count in its favour that any thought experiment that sought to challenge it would meet considerable difficulty in maintaining that the imagined experience in question was a genuinely sensory one. Furthermore, if something of that unexpected sort could be imagined, it would clearly be difficult to do so except parasitically on the back of experience that was unequivocally spatio-temporal in nature. Absolutely original a-spatial, a-temporal, sensory experience seems not to be a possibility, and that is all Kant needs to insist on. The upshot of this is that the *a priori* concepts *space* and *time* and their various derivatives such as *duration succession*, *extent*, *distance* and the rest must be recognized as metaphysically central to experience, and that we must be prepared to understand experience itself in the light of any consequences that are forced on us in the wake of accepting these fundamental ideas' *a priori* character.

'Space is not a discursive, or as we say, general concept of relations of things in general, but a pure intuition' (A24–5/B39). Here we have the principal positive claim that Kant makes to supplement the negative point he takes himself to have just established. It stands in need of considerable unpacking since the thought is densely compressed and its expression dubiously grammatical. What is not a general concept is not so much Space itself, which isn't a concept at all, but the concept *space*. (In case of doubt, we can remind ourselves that the section of the Aesthetic we are here concerned with is labelled 'the Metaphysical Exposition of this *Concept*'.) And if the concept *space* isn't a general one, it must inevitably be singular (on the obvious enough assumption that it isn't syncategorematic). Now singular concepts are concepts of particular things, and the traditional teaching of Kant's day had it, reasonably enough, that such concepts, or ideas, are learned from our experience of the very particulars they stand for, as Locke had illustrated with his talk of the child's ideas *Nurse* and *Mamma* (*Essay*, III.iii.7). In Kantian language, experiential acquaintance with some particular is called 'intuition' of that particular, and by extension, the particular things with which we are experientially acquainted and of which we form singular concepts could easily be spoken of as 'intuitions'. So, as I see you, I have an intuition of you, or I might say in a kind of lax shorthand, you are an intuition of mine. With this in mind, we could envisage Kant reflecting on the Lockean idea *Nurse* and saying that 'Nurse is not a discursive, or as we say, general concept, but an intuition', meaning that the concept *Nurse* is a singular one which stands for and is learnt from acquaintance with a particular individual once present in intuition, to wit, Nurse herself. So it is with the concept *space* at A24–5, only with the crucial difference that whereas the intuition of Nurse is an empirical one, that of Space is not; it is pure, non-empirical, or *a priori* (these three terms being to all intents and purposes interchangeable). And now we have to ask what an *a priori* intuition might be, and how Kant supposes there could be any such thing.

There is no doubt that Kant's text is unsatisfactory at this point. He emphasizes the singularity and uniqueness of Space and the way in which, when we talk of diverse spaces, we have in mind no more than parts of the one all-embracing Space that there is. And he uses that thought to support the claim that 'an *a priori*, and not an empirical, intuition underlies all concepts of space' (A25/B39), which it certainly does not do. One might, after all, rightly or wrongly, think of there being one singular Green, of which all determinate shades are elements, without thereby being persuaded that an *a priori* and non-empirical intuition (of Green) underlies all concepts of green.

Nevertheless, the deficiency at this point in Kant's train of thought can easily enough be ignored, since it is clear enough how he is really moving. We know already that the concept *space* is not empirically acquired. We further know that being singular, it is used to designate an individual of one kind or another. Yet it cannot stand for any particular that happens to be given to us in sensible experience deriving from the manifold of sensation, for (a) there is no such individual, and (b) if there were, the concept would be empirical, and not pure or *a priori* as has already been established. Hence the only possibility that remains is that Space must be given to us as a pure intuition and that it is that which the non-empirical concept *space* designates. That is the formality of Kant's position, only it leaves entirely undisclosed what it is for us to have anything deserving of the title 'an *a priori* intuition' of Space, or of Time (or indeed of anything else, if other *a priori* intuitions there should be). That lacuna urgently demands to be filled.

In talking of intuitions I drew attention to the way in which we (and Kant) find it easy to slide without notice between thought of our experience of some particular thing and thought of the particular thing of which we have that experience. In coming to understand the *a priori* intuition of Space that is a slide on which we can draw. We have already seen that for Kant experience is not identical with the sensibly given manifold of intuition, but is the output of the ways in which we exercise our faculties of mind in making sense of, or, as he puts it, 'synthesizing', that manifold. The singularity of Space then, not being anything internal to the manifold, we can only see it as deriving from the way in which as sensibility-dependent creatures we fashion experience out of the manifold, namely by representing things within a single all-embracing spatio-temporal framework. This framework, which structures our experience, can then be called 'an intuition' in virtue of its singularity, and the intuition that it is is an *a priori* one just because the concept that it allows us to introduce is not empirical, not answerable to elements of experience drawn from the sensory manifolds that are given to us in the flow of our conscious awareness.

A critic might want to protest that he had been led to expect an account of how we come by the concept *space*, and that in being told that Space is an *a priori* intuition, Kant has failed to provide any answer. There is some justice in this complaint, although it is one that can be rectified on Kant's behalf easily enough. When we ask how we come by the concept and are told: 'Not from experience', the inclination is to hear that answer as a promise of something else from which we do learn the concept. And then we are disappointed when nothing else is provided. But Kant should encourage us to suppress that inclination. We don't learn the concept *space* from something other than experience, rather we acquire it through exercising it in ordering the empirical intuitions of our day-to-day experience in its terms. That we do so is a fundamental feature of what it is to be minded in the particular way we are. If our empirical concepts are ones we have to learn before we are able to exercise them, our non-empirical, *a priori* concepts are ones we come by through their very exercise. If there is learning or acquisition involved here that can be nothing other than what goes on as we find ourselves coming freely to exercise capacities that are built into the structure of our minds from the word go. (If this thought seems unpalatable, one might find comfort in comparing the idea to the mundane one of a dog's learning to swim, or a child's learning to ride a bicycle. The dog may well be encouraged by its master and the child by its parent, but in neither case are we obliged to say that there is something or someone from which or from whom they learn what they do.)

The upshot of Kant's reflection then is this. Because *space* and *time* are not empirical concepts and yet are concepts that are necessary for any experiential articulation of the world, we have to recognize that what we are given in sensible intuition must be ordered within a spatio-temporal framework. That framework is the *form* of sensibility, and in consequence of that we should find it entirely natural to think of the world of our experience as the world that appears to us through that absolutely unavoidable *a priori* matrix. What we experience in perception and what eventually the sciences teach us about the world we perceive (whether or not we perceive it as the sciences describe it) can reasonably enough be called in a sort of Kantian shorthand 'appearance', and it need not estrange us unduly to find him constantly speaking of the objects of our perceptual experience in this way as appearances, as *Erscheinungen*.

Before we can feel entirely at ease with this way of speaking, two things need to be added. The first is that our own use of the word 'appearance' often brings with it the suggestion of a contrast with reality: 'It only appears to be raining'; 'He's not really sulking, he only appears to be'. If that were the usage Kant had in mind, then clearly he would already have stumbled badly on his way to resolving the sceptical troubles of his predecessors. But the German word '*Erscheinung*' that Kant uses carries no such overtones. (That job is done instead by a word Kant does not use, to wit, '*Schein*'.) So just as for us things can appear to be as they really are, so too for Kant appearances can and often do reveal the world that presents itself to us as it in fact is. Only there is this difference from our usual way of thinking, namely, that the world that presents itself to us as it really is presents itself to us through the *a priori* forms of intuition that reflect the fundamental nature of our minds. Those forms, however, import no distortion into our perceptual judgement. The ideas of distortion and its absence, the ideas of our perceiving things aright or not, are ideas which only have their application *within* those forms, hence *within* the realm of 'appearances'. To suppose otherwise would be to misunderstand Kant's position in a particularly crass way.

The second thing to insist on now is that although I have already introduced the entirely Kantian distinction between the world as it appears and the world as it is in itself, there is nothing in the argument I have been outlining that gives us reason to think that the world that presents itself to us in appearance is any different from the world as it is in itself. The reason should be plain. As I have represented Kant's thinking, the concepts in terms of which I order my perceptual experience cannot all be acquired in the way of Locke's simple ideas just by noticing recurrent features of the perceptual flow (the manifold of intuition) and then judging how things are in their terms. In addition there are non-empirical, *a priori* concepts, and when they are concepts that we are bound to use whatever shape our experience comes to take, they are formal or transcendental ones. With its focus on the exiguous character of the manifold of intuition this line of thought tells us nothing about the world, so it tells us nothing about the world as it is in itself, independently of us and our ways of experiencing it. So, as we come to feel at home with Kant's speaking of the world that experience reveals to us as the world of appearance, we should remember that further argument is needed before we are forced to the conclusion that epitomizes Transcendental Idealism, the conclusion that experience can give us no knowledge of the world as it is in itself and that about it we must resign ourselves to ignorance.

There are two negative theses here that it is useful to distinguish, though in fact Kant accepted both. One is that things in themselves could not be spatio-temporally disposed, related to one another in each of four dimensions, or more cautiously and leaving open whether the in-itself really embraces countable items, that the in-itself enjoys no spatio-temporal determination of any sort. The other is that even if that were a possibility for the in-itself, no experience we could have would yield knowledge of that aspect of it, it being at best a reality that we might ignorantly mirror, but not knowingly represent.

From Kant's viewpoint, as here presented, it does appear that both theses will be true, the second holding indeed just because the first one does. We know that when we speak of Space and Time we are using singular concepts which refer to the ordering framework to which the bare manifold of intuition is input. General spatial and temporal concepts such as *broad, long, together, simultaneous* and the like are essentially dependent on our *a priori* intuition of that armature, and have no sense independently of that. So at least we must assume, in want of Kant's saying anything else about them.[5] Now, if we ask whether the world as it is in itself is, or even might be, spatially and temporally disposed, that question can only be framed using the singular concepts *space* and *time*. But for Kant those concepts can have no other sense than that they refer to what they do refer to, viz., the ordering framework we bring to the manifold in the synthesis of experience. Their sense cannot be detached from that just in virtue of their being singular concepts and not general ones. Hence the question that is being entertained effectively takes the form of asking whether the world as it is on its own account and independent of us could be of a kind that is essentially dependent on us. The very supposition embodies a contradiction, so the answer to the question must be 'No', and not just as a contingent matter of fact, but of necessity. It follows immediately that if that is the answer, it could not be the case that we should just be inevitably ignorant of its actual spatio-temporal character.

Of course we are tempted to think that no such argument can go through just because for us temporal and spatial notions appear to make no essential reference to ourselves. So we suppose there is no evident contradiction in talking about the speed of light or the size of the nearest galaxy in ways that make no allusion, even indirectly, to ourselves and our mental structure. But that is just to forget that for Kant it is already unshakeably established that the crucial notions are *a priori* ones and that he would feel entirely justified in reproving us for overlooking that. Once we hold that teaching of his firmly in place we shall see that that will affect the way in which we are able to construe those derivative spatio-temporal notions that pervade our experience and in terms of which the contents of our world are ordered. To Kant's way of thinking, our ordinary modes of talking in this area need to be revised or at least reinterpreted from bottom to top.

Not that we find Kant himself speaking like that. He himself offers different considerations altogether to get to the conclusion that the world in itself could not be spatial or temporal, notably arguments that depend on what he sees as the necessity of Euclidean geometry and the necessity of elementary arithmetical propositions. However, those arguments are usually found wanting, and what I have done here on Kant's behalf is merely to extract the consequence he wanted directly from the apriority and the singularity of the concepts *space* and *time*. The detour through the philosophy of mathematics is strictly speaking superfluous, although I shall say a little about it in a moment.

It may be thought that there is inconsistency in Kant's view at this point though, since he is repeatedly insistent that we can and do know nothing of the world as it is in itself. Yet is he not pretending to know – either via the mathematical route that I have left unexplored, or by means of the short-cut I have offered in its place – something negative about the world in itself, viz. that it is a-spatial and a-temporal? The answer is 'Yes', Kant does think he knows that, but that is an acquisition of pure reason, not of experience, and when he is careful, the admission of necessary ignorance about the in-itself extends only to knowledge that can be acquired empirically. That later on in the *Critique*, in the Tran-scendental Dialectic, Kant is concerned to show how philosophy has traditionally failed to respect the limitations there are to the proper exercise of pure reason and to identify mistakes that have been made in drawing metaphysical conclusions about the world as it is in itself from the apparent teachings of reason does not show that reason has absolutely nothing to teach us about the world. There is no inconsistency in Kant's position at this point.

A while back I said that the *a priori* concepts of space and time should be thought of as expressing the fundamental structure of the sensibility-dependent mind. That, for Kant, is the only serious alternative to their being empirical concepts. One may wonder whether that is not to overlook an obvious continuity between the innateness of these ideas as embraced by Kant's continental predecessors, Descartes and Leibniz, and what Kant himself is proposing. Kant firmly denies this, and we can see now why. Traditionally, ideas were taken to be innately given by God to human minds to enable them to acquire knowledge that they would otherwise be incapable of articulating. In Descartes' case, it is the innateness of the apparently singular concept *God* that makes for our knowledge of God's existence and in other cases secures ideas' resembling features of things that our sensory input singularly fails to do. In that of Leibniz, without innate conceptual stock, monads' metaphysical insulation from causal contact with one another and the world they make up would leave them, and so us, entirely ignorant of it. In both cases the assumption is that God provides us with such ideas innately to reveal what the world is like in itself, and we have seen why Kant thinks that must be a nonsense. As far as the empirically accessible world goes, we have no need of miraculous aids to its comprehension; introspection, everyday experience and the natural sciences cover the field. If our formal ideas of space and time were innate, because they would have to be viewed as revealing the world as it is in itself, they would of necessity fail in their function, representing it erroneously, not truly. On the assumption of God's omniscience and benevolence, His giving us the ideas of space and time innately is then something He is bound not to do, lest, rather than instruct us, they lead us astray. (Kant's brief discussion of the innateness hypothesis is at B167–8.)

Strictly speaking, Transcendental Idealism is the purely negative doctrine that we have no experiential knowledge of the world as it is in itself, and that claim has not been fully established yet even with respect to sensibility, which is all that Kant is concerned with in the Aesthetic. We may accept that Space and Time are transcendentally ideal, viz. not things in themselves or features of the in-itself, but there is much that sensibility reveals that we would not dream of assimilating to either of them. Just to note that these other things are appearances does not, surely, rule them out as appearances of the world in itself. The argument needs to be completed at this point, and to do that we have only to exploit material already to hand.

The necessity of space and time was introduced at first as arising from the contents of our sensory awareness all having a spatial or temporal dimension (or both). Nothing that is given to us in sensibility fails to find its place in the framework within which we order our experience. Now the non-spatio-temporal features of things we are aware of in sensibility such as, say, their delicacy or their inevitability and the like, will be, directly or indirectly, features of things that are themselves spatio-temporally situated, and as such not be things in themselves. Consequently their non-spatio-temporal qualities will also fail to be features of things in themselves. If those things are called appearances, these non-spatio-temporal properties and relations will hold of, or be determinations of, appearances only. With that, the argument is as complete as it can be made and, I think, as complete as Kant has any interest in making it.

I have already warned against one misunderstanding of 'appearance', effectively the confusion of *Erscheinung* with *Schein*. More has to be said before the concept is apt to express Kant's own form of empirical realism, the positive epistemic doctrine, logically independent of Transcendental Idealism, that, while we can have no knowledge of the world as it is in itself, we do have knowledge of the world as it appears.[6] At first sight, we might think Kant is merely saying that while experience cannot teach us what the world is like in itself, we do at least know how it appears to us. But that is far too weak for his purpose, since it effectively does no more than echo the kind of view expressed by Descartes and by Locke, who had no doubt about how things appeared to them in perception, but were puzzled about our right to claim knowledge about what it was in the world that appeared to us in that familiar way. Since Kant is ambitious to progress beyond the point at which they stalled, his use of 'appearance' must be far sturdier than theirs.

The suggestion I lightly sketched towards the end of the last chapter should serve this end, if only it can be given a little more filling. Experience of spatio-temporally located individuals is experience of individuals that do presumably have a character of their own (in themselves, that is), but which character cannot but elude us.[7] However, they also have propensities to display themselves in ways that are peculiar to perceivers who access them via the various forms of experience their mental constitution obliges them to deploy. Then, when that mental equipment is being used aright it may well detect a truth about the world, namely that it is of a kind to be experienced as (*scilicet*, to appear) thus and so. It can be seen straightway that this way of putting Kant's idea is distinct from the weak doctrine just rejected, for according to that weak view, experience would reveal how the world appears to me simply in virtue of its seeming to me that things are thus and so, whether or not I was deploying my senses aright. By contrast, according to the stronger version, my experience will only knowledgeably reveal the world providing that I am respecting the appropriate canons of sound judgement about what confronts me and also that what confronts me also has its in-itself character, one that impinges upon me in the appearances to which it gives rise. Nevertheless, Kant will say, we have to recognize that in those circumstances we should not suppose ourselves to know anything other about the world than the appearances it presents to us.

One signal advantage of understanding Kant's brand of realism in this way is that it frees us from any temptation to think of him as ultimately committing himself to an extravagant 'two worlds' doctrine, worlds which are quite unconnected with one another, one of which is shot through with spatio-temporality, and the other of which rigorously excludes it.[8] The drive to that understanding of Kant's thought is that otherwise it may seem that he runs into contradiction: no world can possess contradictory properties, yet the world of appearance is spatio-temporal and the world in itself is not. Hence, it seems, he must suppose there to be two logically independent worlds. The construal of 'appearance' offered here, however, avoids all need for such a move. As it appears to us, the world is spatio-temporal in nature, whereas considered in itself it is not. Here there is only one world, thought about in these different ways from different points of view. As Kant puts it at Bxxvii, a distinction is made 'between things as objects of experience and *those same things* as things in themselves' (my emphasis). To say that from one point of view the world is *F* and from another it is not-*F* imports no contradiction. Nor does it import any intellectual extravagance beyond what we have met already.[9]

Nevertheless, it might be thought that I am committing Kant to more than he wants, and in a way which is reminiscent of one strand of Berkeley's philosophy, which, in general, Kant firmly rejects. On his way to his own brand of idealism, Berkeley had argued that there was no sound distinction to be drawn between primary qualities and secondaries, between those properties that things possess in their own right and those which we essentially explain in terms of the ways they strike us in perception. (Indeed, he further denies any distinction between qualities and ideas of qualities, so assimilating primary qualities not to secondary qualities, but to *ideas* of secondary qualities, with the further consequence that there are simply no qualities left for substance to possess (*First Dialogue between Hylas and Philonous*).) Now, as I have presented Kant, it will seem that he, too, is assimilating primary qualities (spatio-temporal properties and those that are implicitly spatial or temporal) to secondaries, for the introduction of space and time as *a priori* forms of intuition has the implication that what we are perceptually sensitive to can only be understood through our peculiar mode of awareness. Yet at A29/B45 Kant explicitly rejects the view that he is 'supposing that the ideality of space (i.e. its failure to determine the world as it is in itself) can be illustrated by examples so altogether insufficient as colours, taste etc.' So, it can seem that in the interpretation I have offered of his thought is traduced, not accurately presented.

The response to this objection must be to acknowledge that this reading of Kant does indeed present him as understanding the traditional primary qualities as fundamentally secondary in nature, but to deny that it does so in the way that he himself understands those qualities. That is far more like what Berkeley took them to be than what they really are, viz. as *ideas* of secondary qualities, not as secondary *qualities* proper. In this way, Kant rejects the comparison of his view of space with colour and taste, because 'these cannot rightly be regarded as properties of things, but only as changes in the subject, changes which may, indeed, be different for different men' (A29/B45). Only, here he displays a mistaken understanding of what colour and taste are, and rashly concurs with Berkeley's assimilation of them to ideas of qualities (or to appearances in the last rejected sense). To see that this is a mistake we have only to reflect that it can be a perfectly informative answer to the question 'Why does this jam taste so sweet?' to reply 'Because it *is* that sweet', thus assuring our questioner that he isn't suffering from some momentary breakdown in his sense of taste. Were the Kantian view of the matter correct, however, that answer itself could only be construed as saying 'Because the jam tastes so sweet', hence in no way as going beyond the information already provided by the question. Once Kant is set right about this, going by his lights he no longer has grounds for rejecting a properly secondary quality construal of his 'transcendental concept of appearances in space' (A30/B45).[10]

Anyone who finds the comparison between Kant's transcendental construction of space and time and secondary quality experience illuminating will find it natural to draw on it to explain why the world in itself could not enjoy any spatio-temporal character. Presumably the world in itself has to have some features or other of its own if only in order that there be some ultimately explanatory ground of the world being accessible to us in appearance. As Kant puts it in the Preface to the *Critique*'s second edition, at Bxxvi, 'although we cannot *know* these objects as things in themselves, we must yet be in position to *think* them as things in themselves; otherwise we should be landed in the absurd conclusion that there can be appearances without anything that appears'.[11] These features of the world in itself will be analogous to primary qualities in that to any mind that comprehends them (a mind like God's, say, that enjoys intellectual, though not sensible, intuition) they will be explicable without allusion to any particular point of view from which they are apprehended. Since it has been argued that this cannot be the case for the spatio-temporal nature of things, it again follows directly that the world in itself could not be spatio-temporal in character, only unknowably so as far as we are concerned.

The arguments I have just outlined are not ones that Kant explicitly uses (quite apart from his wayward understanding of colour and taste). His own preferred route to the same conclusion is entirely different, and depends on a logical doctrine that I have not yet mentioned. Because it is of such general importance to Kant's overall thought, it demands presentation in its own right, and since it also serves in his mind by itself to exclude the presence of spatio-temporality from the realm of the in-itself, it will be convenient to close this chapter with notice of it.

I have discussed Kant's thought about sensible intuition in the Transcendental Aesthetic without pausing over his own Introduction, which sets out the structure for the whole *Critique*. This is largely concerned with the division of assertions we make into those that are necessary and those that are not, with the division of our knowledge between what is *a priori* (independent of experience) and *a posteriori* (authenticated in one way or another through experience). The largest segment of *a priori* knowledge is provided, Kant believes, by assertions that are trivial in that they do no more than unpack the content of their subject terms in their predicates. Thus 'All vixens are female foxes' is an instance of *a priori* knowledge of this kind because our grasp of it depends on nothing other than the possession of the concepts *vixen*, *female* and *fox*, and a recognition that the last two are already involved in the first. Propositions that express this trivial sort of *a priori* knowledge Kant calls 'analytic'.

By contrast, propositions knowledge of whose truth requires appeal to experience of the world, such as 'Vixens in cub are ferocious', or 'Buildings that are undermined collapse', Kant calls 'synthetic'. Our knowledge of these *a posteriori* truths does not just elucidate or explicate their subject terms in the way analytic propositions do; it amplifies our understanding of what falls under those terms. Now, Kant takes it that there is room for a third type of proposition, straddling the two already picked out, a kind of proposition that is not dependent on experience for ratification, but which is anything but trivial in its content. Such propositions are not analytic, but synthetic; and yet they are *a priori*, not *a posteriori*. Everything in the *Critique* that follows this Introduction is ordered around the question whether there can be any genuine synthetic *a priori* knowledge, and if so, how it is possible. Certainly, traditional metaphysics, concerned largely with the soul, God and freedom, purported to establish substantive *a priori* truths about the world, and, as I have already said, a large part of the *Critique* is given over to showing that such claims are unsustainable. On the other hand, it seems that reviewing the material in the Aesthetic discussed so far, we find that there are compelling claims overlooked by traditional metaphysics which enjoy that same synthetic *a priori* status as those overblown ones, yet which cannot be dismissed as illusory. One such that we have already met is that all our sensible experience is of a spatio-temporally ordered world. Another is that the experienced world makes up a unified and infinitely extended spatial and temporal whole. A third is that all consciousness takes place in time.

Kant's question then about such non-trivial *a priori* knowledge is how it is possible, and he thinks we are already in possession of the materials needed to supply the answer. Such propositions are not *a posteriori* because they do not answer to the matter of experience that the world happens to throw up. They are quite universal in that everyone is rationally bound to assent to them no matter what their experience is like; we are compelled to accept them, like it or not. In that sense they are necessary, and because we can see that independently of any experience we have, they are known *a priori*. But their necessity is not the formal necessity of analytic truths, since if it were, these propositions would not be as substantial as they are, but merely trivial. What accounts for their *a priori* status, on Kant's view, is that they reflect directly or indirectly, fixed truths about the *form* of experience in so far as that is determined by the very nature of our minds. That and, he thinks, that alone will explain why they are synthetic. The explanation of such propositions' truth and their claim to our assent is that they record aspects of (or consequences of) the way our mental framework fixes the character of our experience and the world as we know it. Apart from that, as Kant will argue later on in the case of traditional speculative metaphysics, there can only be the illusion of synthetic *a priori* knowledge.

Against this background, we can understand Kant's own way of arguing that the world as it is in itself could not be a spatio-temporal world, even unbeknownst to us. There are, he thinks, notable truths relating to space and time which are incontestably synthetic *a priori* in character. Such are the truths of geometry in the one case, and of arithmetic in the other, truths which are *a priori* in that they do not depend on experience for their ratification, but which are none the less not just trivial amplifications of the concepts we use to express them, which would make them analytic. But if propositions such as 'the shortest distance between two points is a straight line' or '$7 + 5 = 12$' are indeed synthetic and *a priori*, the truths they express must answer to their dependence on formal features of our world, not its matter. Only then can we explain why they are neither trivial nor contingent, but have the curiously informative necessity that they do. If they really did express truths about the world in itself, they would have to be material truths, and hence contingent ones. Since that is not what they are, we are bound to conclude that those propositions that articulate them can only apply to the world as it presents itself to us, and that what lies beyond that not only lies outside our ken but also beyond our powers of precise articulation. That is, if we thought to articulate something about the world in itself using the language of geometry, we should fail to do so, since any truth we might express could only be a synthetic *a priori* truth: but then it could not be a truth about anything other than the world as it appears. Furthermore, we could not even truly say that the world in itself might be somehow closely analogous to the spatio-temporal world of appearance, since any attempt to spell out the analogy would need to do so in a way that appeared to express a truth, and the truth that it expressed would have to appear as a synthetic *a priori* one, again reflecting the world as it appears and not as it is in itself.

These last paragraphs condense intricate and contentious material (A7–10/B10–19; A 46–9/B 64–6). To expand them would require asking how sympathetic we can be to Kant's division of our knowledge into the synthetic *a posteriori*, the analytic *a priori* and the synthetic *a priori*. We should also have to ask whether we can accept that truths of mathematics really do belong in the latter class and whether there is the close connection Kant purports to find between our grasp of geometry and arithmetic and the two forms of sensibility that dominate our experience. I shall not embark on these issues here. My purpose in introducing them has solely been to expound the main lines of Kant's own way of thinking about sensibility, and that I have now done. Before going on, however, it will be helpful to draw together the main points that Kant takes himself to have established by the end of the Transcendental Aesthetic. These are:

a) Our sensible experience of the world, be that of our own inner states or of things other than ourselves, is immutably ordered in space or time, or both.
b) That truth is fixed by the nature of sensibility itself, and it is not something that sensible experience could ever falsify.
c) It is a consequence of (a) and (b) that the world we experience cannot be the world as it is in itself, independent of its relation to us and to our minds.

d) Not being the world as it is in itself, what presents itself to us in intuition can only be the world as it is related to us, to wit, the world as it appears.

e) Sensible intuition gives us immediate and non-inferential access to the world as it appears.[12]

f) To accept (a)–(e) is to possess the key to resolving the epistemological difficulties inherited from the late seventeenth and mid-eighteenth centuries.

Notice, though, that at no point has it been asserted that sensible intuition taken by itself amounts to knowledge, not even knowledge of the world as it appears. The point may be put by saying that as far as the Aesthetic goes, we can see that it is not ruled out that sensible intuition should put us on the path to attaining experiential knowledge of the world (as it appears), but that this is more than one possibility among others has yet to be shown. In taking himself to have discovered the key to the problems that beset his predecessors, Kant well knows he has not yet shown how that key turns the lock. This is matter for the next section of the *Critique*, the Transcendental Analytic, to which we can now turn.

3

Experience and Judgement: The Metaphysical Deduction

We order the world that sensibility presents to us within the framework of space and time. To that extent the world of our experience is of our own making, only erroneously thought of as the world as it is in itself. Properly speaking, it is the world of appearance, both in its inner and its outer aspects. For all the seeming amplitude of these claims, it would be a mistake to have an exaggerated view of what Kant takes himself to have established in the *Critique*'s early pages.

I have loosely spoken of sensibility as having a content and even, more grandly, as passively presenting a world to us, but it would be premature to think of this world as already fitted out with objects of the kinds we are most familiar with, domestic pets, say, or the jumbled items in a shopping bag, let alone with the atoms and the particles of the physical sciences or the nearby planets and the distant stars. All the term 'world' stretches to so far is whatever it is that sensibility *alone* provides, and even the identification of such material as *objects* takes us well beyond that. The very idea of an object involves its existing independently of our awareness of it, and that is something to which outer sense does not attest by itself, even as it presents to us something other than ourselves. In fact, it would be exaggerating the role of sensible intuition even to say that through it alone we find ourselves presented with a world of individual things at all, since that thought inevitably brings with it the idea of some classification of what the senses offer us, *as* a domestic pet or *as* the various individual items of shopping in the bag. To Kant, it is quite clear that that classifying task falls not to sensibility, but to the understanding, and about that nothing has yet been said.

So, the positive achievement of the Aesthetic scarcely reaches any further than to the recognition that the representations and appearances of sense have to be ordered in space and time.[1] Put like that, we can see that philosophy's preoccupation with our right to claim experiential knowledge of a world of objects distinct from our minds, persisting through time and accessible to investigation by the natural sciences, is virtually untouched. What we do have, though, is the overarching thought that if it should prove possible to put that traditionally desiderated, yet elusive, material in place, we shall have to do so within a spatio-temporal framework, since in our case the understanding has to apply itself first and foremost to what sensibility provides.[2] The transcendental, *a priori*, nature of that matrix will constrain any further substantive material Kant may be able to put in place as he comes to attend to the second fundamental faculty of the mind involved in fashioning our experience. Understanding, then, is the topic of that part of the *Critique* that follows the Aesthetic and which Kant called 'Transcendental Analytic'.[3] The analysis that is in question here, he tells us, is not that of any particular concepts, rather it is the dissection of the very faculty of understanding itself, and it has as its prime aim the location of *a priori* elements that it imports into our experience akin to the *a priori* forms of sensibility already discussed (A65–6/B90–1).

To many of Kant's predecessors it would have seemed idle to talk about the understanding at this point. By and large, the assumption had been that our experience consists of nothing other than strings and arrays of images, impressions or sensations that we are presented with in sensibility. Our intellectual problems stem from the difficulty of wanting to read into these strings and arrays more than they already comprise. If only Kant had recognized that, they might have said, he could have confined his investigations to sensibility, and then have admitted that there was no further progress to be made beyond what the previous century had achieved. In rejecting this complaint Kant had a retort that in effect changed the course that philosophy took, and which consisted in overturning the established imagistic conception of experience. In its place he proposed something that makes him an entirely modern thinker while his forerunners now strike us, in this respect at least, rather more like antiquated curiosities.[4]

The crucial insight that moves Kant at this point is that our experience is through and though *propositional*, not imagistic. That is, we do not have experience by having image-like representations of things one after another; rather, on the basis of what is provided by sensibility, by means of the understanding we fashion judgements to the effect *that something is the case*. So, for example, my present sensible experience is experience *that* the books on the desk are scattered loosely around, *that* the dogs are comfortably stretched out before the fire, *that* you are looking rather pale this morning and so on. And in taking this step of viewing experience as essentially propositional, Kant makes it plain that understanding is ineliminably in play whenever the mind makes active sense of the manifold data that sensibility passively serves up.

Even if we did think of the deliverances of sensibility as some kind of image, Kant would be quite right to insist that such images are only something for us, something through which the world is present to us in consciousness, provided that we identify their content in thought *as* of this or that, *as* of a couple of dogs, *as* of a pile of books, *as* of a friend, and so on. Then, in addition, our identification of what is so given only reveals the world to us through displaying *how* those dogs, those books, that friend are, *how* they should be thought of, that is, *as* stretched out comfortably by the fire, *as* scattered about on the desk, *as* looking pale, etcetera. Only when these entirely new elements, supplied by the understanding, are taken into account will it be at all plausible to say that what sensibility provides us with amounts to experience. Philosophy cannot avoid stepping out into this new terrain.

The upshot, then, is that we shall only come to a decent account of experience if we recognize that it involves our actively classifying and ordering the passively received data of sensation. Ordering and classifying the sensory manifold is what Kant calls 'combining' or 'synthesizing' it in judgement, and this synthesis is the proper defining activity of the understanding. We may be passive receptors of the manifold of intuition, but as far as its synthesis goes, we are, through the engagement of understanding, active and spontaneous. Without the input of sensibility there would be nothing for the understanding to operate on, that is true enough and agreed on all hands; but likewise, and this is novel, without the active operation of the understanding and its spontaneous deployment of descriptive and classificatory concepts, sensibility would be unrevealing. As Kant puts it in one of the most famous and most often quoted phrases of the whole *Critique*: 'Thoughts without content are empty, intuitions without concepts are blind' (A51/B75).

Philosophers like Locke, or Hume, might suppose that they have already accommodated this particular thought, or at least believe that they could easily do so. If pressed, Locke might be happy enough to allow that we do not enjoy fully-fledged experience until we have formed ideas of sensation or of reflection, and Hume too might agree that the flow of impressions only produces experience to the extent that it is captured by ideas, where the term 'ideas' in either case corresponds to Kant's 'concepts'. However, even if this were accepted – and in truth it stretches charity to do so, since there is plenty of evidence in Locke's 1690 *Essay* and in Hume's 1745 *Treatise of Human Nature* to support the thought that they conceived of experience as the sensory flow itself, identical with the Kantian manifold of intuition, and that they supposed reflection and

thought about the sensory flow to be something over and above experience – even then, Kant would still insist that something had escaped them
both, and something which is of central importance. This is that those
elements out of which classical empiricism constructed its understanding
of experience, in addition to bringing the elements of sensation under
concepts, need to be supplemented by an account of how those various
conceptualized elements fit together as discrete wholes.

As I see a red kite flying above me in the park, and experience the
world in those terms, more must be going on than that the conceptualized item of *redness* is concatenated with a conceptualized item *kite* and
then further concatenated with the items *above* and *me* and *the park*. Not
only is no mention of order made in the empiricist picture, so that the
redness belongs together with the kite rather than with me or with the
park; more important still, nothing is said that would tell us what makes
some selections of elements proper to represent some experience while
others plainly are not (as, for example, the mere concatenation of *redness*
and *above*). Putting it in a way that Kant would find congenial, what is
entirely lacking in previous centuries' thought about the subject is any
sense of what constitutes the *unity* internal to our various experiences
taken one by one. This, Kant thinks, can only be provided by reflection
on the way the understanding operates as it brings the manifold of
sensation under concepts in complete judgements.

A good way of capturing the distance between Kant and the earlier
thinkers, then, would be to say that whereas they either equated experience with the passively received manifold of intuition itself, or, more
generously, with some sort of elementary conceptualization of it, for
Kant, experience is nothing less than the output of our actively ordering
and combining the manifold in judgements to the effect that things stand
thus and so in space and time. The manifold itself is quite distinct from
anything he would recognize as experience proper, while for his predecessors, even on the larger view, there is practically no distance between
the two. As Kant expresses himself at A69/B94, 'We can reduce all acts of
the understanding to judgement, and the understanding may therefore be
represented as a faculty of judgement.' These words signal the advance
that Kant's concentration on the understanding fundamentally brought
with it.

To appreciate the centrality of judgement, it suffices to reflect that in
experience, we represent the world. Consequently, the unity that every
experience must enjoy will be one that allows it to be assessed as true or
false. In Kant's eyes, what can be assessed as true or false are judgements.
Consequently, he takes it that understanding must operate in the fashioning of experience not just by bringing the manifold of sensible intuition

under concepts, but by doing so *in the form of judgements*, and, *a fortiori*, in the various forms of judgement that there are. So, for example, in experiencing the sun as shining I can be thought of as combining the given manifold of intuition using the concept *the sun* and then bringing that conceptualized intuition under the further concept *shining*. This I do in a judgement that is assessable as true or false and which will inevitably be cast in one or other of the various forms marked out in the formal study of logic. In this particular case my experience is that the sun is shining, and articulated in a judgement of subject – predicate form, one which Kant calls 'assertoric', 'singular' and 'categorical'.

Thus, at this early point in the discussion of the faculty of understanding, we have already found something to match the formal role of space and time in sensible intuition.[5] Just as all experience that draws on sensibility subjects its contents to the framework that that brings with it, so, as we employ the understanding in fashioning representations out of the sensibly given manifold, we are obliged to do so in whatever ways are implicit in bringing those contents under the sorts of judgements that are available to us. In the Metaphysical Exposition of the Concepts *Space* and *Time*, Kant had emphasized the *necessity* of those *a priori* representations as ones we could not dispense with. It was a basic and unalterable fact about ourselves that we are dependent on sensibility for the experience we have. So there is a dual necessity here, first that our experience be sensible, and then secondly that sensible experience be spatio-temporal. Now, at the start of the Analytic, we find a similar duality, this time concerning the understanding. It is a basic and unalterable fact about ourselves that we are dependent on the exercise of understanding in fashioning experience out of the passively given manifold; then, it is a further necessity that the exercise of understanding cannot be detached from combining representations (intuitions and concepts) in the form of judgements. So just as our experience must be spatio-temporal in its form, so too it must be structured in the various ways that propositional judgement brings with it.

For Kant these are absolute truths about ourselves and about the knowledge of the world we can come to through experience, but just as was the case with sensibility, where there could be intuition without the exercise of concepts, there is room in logical space for existence of subjects whose representations of the world are independent of sensible input. Their world would not be one that they discursively represent in the way judgement obliges us to represent it. Whether such beings exist in fact is not something about which we can sensibly speculate, though Kant does suppose that angels and God might exercise 'intellectual intuition' and possess a direct non-sensible grasp of the world as it is in itself. At B71 he does expressly deny that God might think (presumably, discursively), since that brings with it inevitable limitation, which is, I surmise, in effect the limitation that the judgements involved in discursive thought tie the thinker inexorably to the world of appearance. He also suggests, at one point, that divine 'intuition' will be less cognitive than creative, possibly also for the same reason (B138–9).

Setting 'intellectual intuition' on one side, Kant also allows for the exercise of discursive understanding by other possible beings whose intuition is quite unlike ours, which he sometimes dubs 'non-sensible'. However, while their experience would not be spatio-temporal, it would none the less be receptive, as God's is not, and depend on quasi-sensible intuition for its content. Their vision of the world will consequently, like ours, be of the world as it appears; only, naturally enough, as it appears to them and not as it appears to us. We shall have occasion later on to ask whether this possibility has consequences for the presumed objectivity of our own grasp of the world's reality and character.

These preliminary thoughts now permit the following speculation. We know that we can speak of sensibility as possessing both *form* and *matter*. Further, we know that concentration on its form secures for us certain *a priori* truths about the character that the experienced world has to take in appearance. So, Kant thinks we may now surmise that understanding too has its formal side, and that that will oblige us to recognize further transcendental constraints on the sort of experience we are able to have, constraints that are additional to those already identified as stemming from sensibility and which derive from the ways in which we are formally obliged to bring the manifold of sensibility under concepts in judgement about it. These too we may suppose to be *a priori* and necessary features of experience. Moreover, and in analogy to what we already know about space and time, if only it could be shown that the very notions which previous generations had found so difficult to secure for experience – objectivity, substancehood, causation, inductive regularity and the like – belong together with the formal aspects of the understanding, then, subject only to the reservation that the experienced world is the world of appearance and not the world as it is in itself, a pathway will be open to the eventual resolution of the outstanding epistemological problems of the previous generations. In a nutshell, developing the Copernican revolution in philosophy within the domain of understanding promises resolution of the scandal of philosophy that Kant confessed had shaken him so badly (Bxxxix fn.).

After introducing this novel and more realistic propositional conception of experience in his introductory remarks about transcendental logic, Kant moves on to identify what he sees as the pure, or formal, concepts of the understanding and which, in homage to Aristotle, he also calls 'categories'. These are concepts which parallel the formal intuitions of space and time that govern the operation of sensibility. Seeing what is going on now as roughly mirroring the earlier discussion of sensibility, we shall expect to find Kant persuading his readers that these concepts are *a priori* ones, and not empirical. Then, he will want to establish that they are also necessary in the sense that we cannot but draw on them in the experience we have of the world. Finally, he must make out that they have their application for us only to things as they appear, and not as they are in themselves. While this is not quite the overt structure of Kant's argument in the text, it will make it easier to grasp its very great intricacies if we bear in mind this underlying, and now familiar, pattern of enquiry.

The passages of the Analytic we have to come to grips with here are three in number. The first is called 'The Clue to the Discovery of All Pure Concepts of the Understanding' (A66–95/B91–129). In it we have the echo of the earlier Metaphysical Exposition of the concepts *space* and *time*, whose principal task it was to exhibit those concepts as *a priori* and not empirical (A23/B38). This passage Kant himself refers to at B159 as the 'metaphysical deduction' of the *a priori* origin of the categories. Secondly, there is the 'Transcendental Deduction of the Pure Concepts of Understanding' (A95–130/B130–69) echoing the earlier Transcendental Exposition in which Kant showed how our dependence on the forms of space and time each impose their own substantial formal constraints on whatever we intuit. The third passage, the 'Schematism of the Pure Concepts of Understanding' (A137–47/B176–87), is not an echo or mirror of the earlier discussion at all, but concerns the way in which the results of the discussion of formal elements of the understanding impinge on what we are given in sensibility. I shall take these three passages in turn, devoting attention to the first two in this chapter and the next, and talking about the third only in conjunction with the immediately following Principles of Pure Understanding (A148–235/B187–294) in chapter 5.

The Metaphysical Deduction

In the Aesthetic Kant had no difficulty identifying the formal elements of sensibility. We are constantly, involuntarily, unavoidably and obviously presented with the spatio-temporal framework within which we order our sensory experience. However, as we turn away from sense and focus now on understanding, things are not so straightforward. We are looking to find some conceptual elements of experience internal to the idea of judgement itself, and nothing presents itself there as being quite so constant, involuntary, unavoidable or obvious. Nevertheless, we have already met one ubiquitous notion that informs our various experiences singly and which had previously escaped notice. This is their peculiar unity. That is nothing other than the fact that in the judgements which articulate our experiences we combine the various empirical elements we are given in ways that can be assessed as true or false. My experience was as of a red kite flying above me in the park, and the various conceptual elements of the judgement that express that experience of mine fit together in a way that ensures my experience represents the world correctly (or, alternatively, misrepresents it).

Kant himself entitled this section of the *Critique* 'The Clue to the Discovery of All Pure Concepts of the Understanding'.[6] I take it that the 'clue', or closer to the German, the 'guiding thread',[7] that Kant had in mind is just this: that as we think about the various ways in which the judgements that articulate our experience acquire their unity, we shall find ourselves coming upon *a priori* concepts that play the same role for the understanding as space and time do for sensibility. These will be concepts without the use of which it would be impossible to experience the world at all, not just contingent ones that reflect what our experience happens to be like. They will be transcendental ones that the understanding is bound to draw on no matter how the world is arranged. To identify them we have only to reflect on judgement itself and understand how Kant thinks of that.

The general picture Kant offers of judging something is that of bringing one representation under another (A68–9/B93). His term 'representation' ranges over both intuitions and concepts, and the simplest case of judgement is one in which something given in intuition is brought under a singular concept, as perhaps in the judgements 'That is our cat' or 'There goes Nurse'. Slightly more complex judgements bring an item that is already thought of under one concept, *F*, under another concept, *G*. So: 'That cat is a greedy animal' or 'Nurse is tired'. Other judgements central to Kant's largely syllogistic logic, such as 'All bodies have weight' or 'Some birds do not sing', are broadly thought of as constructed by bringing representations under representations in other ways. What all experiential judgements have in common though is that the constituent (empirical) representations are so united in our experience that they present something *as being the case*. That is what their unity essentially consists in. And that unity is achieved in one or another of a number of different ways that Kant sets out in the Table of Judgements at A70/B95 and which is reproduced here in figure 3.1.

Quantity of Judgements
Singular (*a* is G)
Particular (Some F is G)
Universal (All Fs are Gs)

Quality	*Relation*
Affirmative (F is G)	Categorical
Negative Not (F is G)	Hypothetical
Infinite (F is not-G)	Disjunctive

Modality
Problematic (it may be the case that *p*)
Assertoric (it is the case that *p*)
Apodeictic (it must be the case that *p*)

Figure 3.1: Kant's 'Table of Judgements' (A70/B95)

To Kant's way of thinking, any judgement that articulates our experience will represent something as being the case through one of the three alternative moments of quality, one of those of quantity, one of relation and one of modality. What determines that an individual judgement has the particular formal features that it does, what makes it a judgement of a particular recurrent form, is that the empirical representations that it contains are connected together by easily identifiable linking concepts that owe nothing to the given empirical manifold and which form a closed list. These entirely formal concepts are laconically set out in the Table of Categories at A81/B106 (see figure 3.2).

There ought be no great puzzlement about the relationship between the individual items on the two tables, and certainly no puzzlement about how Kant gets from the first table to the second. The reason is that what enables him to identify a judgement as one having a particular recurring form can only be the occurrence in its articulation of the clearly identifiable non-empirical and formal concepts that serve to link the given experiential elements in repeatable ways. So, for Kant, what defines a particular form of judgement must be the very concepts that appear in the Table of Categories at the appropriate points. As far as he is concerned, the linkage between the two is analytic and should be entirely perspicuous.

What we have, then, is the idea that on the occasion of experience, generally perceptual, understanding is employed to bring the manifold of

Quantity of Judgements
Unity
Plurality
Totality

Quality
Reality
Negation
Limitation

Relation
Inherence and Subsistence
Causality and Dependence
Community (reciprocity between
agent and patient)

Modality
Possibility–Impossibility
Existence–Non-existence
Necessity–Contingency

Figure 3.2: Kant's 'Table of Categories' (A81/B106)

sensibility together in some unified shape. It does this by connecting the empirically given elements together in judgements of one sort or another. Any judgement represents something or other as being the case, and this is achieved by connecting the conceptualized data of intuition by means of those formal concepts, the categories, that determine the structure of the various forms of judgement that there are. So, to take one simple example, when I perceive the cat as sitting on the mat, I am presented in intuition with some manifold of sensibility that I situate as being outside and distinct from me, and which I conceptualize in terms of the empirical concepts *cat*, *mat* and *sitting*. This I do by connecting them together in the form of a judgement that is singular, affirmative, categorical and assertoric, and that I achieve by combining the various empirically given representations (intuitions or concepts) by means of the categories of unity, reality, inherence and subsistence and contingency. Moreover, since my judgement about the cat is an articulation of my experience, my experience itself will inevitably be informed by these categorial concepts.

To appreciate how these reflections bear upon the contribution made to Transcendental Idealism by the understanding it is not necessary to spend time on the technical detail of Kant's understanding of logic. Obviously enough, its pre-Fregean nature ensures that it will not withstand very close scrutiny today, and concern with issues of logic and logical form were at a significant distance from Kant's metaphysical and epistemological preoccupations. However, anyone sympathetic to Kant's overall programme could quite happily suppose that whatever adjustments are made to the logical machinery with which he operated to bring it up to date would still leave intact the thought that the unity of experience is to be explained in terms of the unity of judgement. The unity of judgement would still be accounted for in terms of the ways in which the empirical elements supplied by intuition are combined to represent something as being the case, and then the logical or formal elements that do the unifying work will still be those that identify the basic forms of judgement that are available to us. With those ideas undisturbed, we can ask how well the main target of the Metaphysical Deduction has been achieved.

First, Kant can say that he has identified one element of experience that has to be attributed to the working of the understanding and is as constantly present as the experiential framework of space and time. That is the element of *something's being the case*. That, we saw, arises out of the empirical data of intuition being combined in accordance with the categories, which we can recognize to be non-empirical *a priori* concepts in either of two ways. First, they are non-empirical, just as the concepts of space and time are non-empirical. They are not concepts that answer to anything given in the manifold of sensation, viewed in the narrow way Kant had inherited that from his predecessors. So, like the concepts *space* and *time*, the categories, and hence, derivatively, the ubiquitous concept of something's being the case, must be presupposed, and so also be *a priori*. Then, secondly, if the putatively pure concepts of the understanding were really empirical concepts, and not pure at all, they would be empirical elements of judgement that would need to be combined to fashion an experiential unity. They could not themselves provide that unity. So, understanding would then have to supply other concepts that served that unifying function, and to avoid regress those concepts would have to be *a priori* ones. Since the listed categorial concepts are precisely those that do supply the unity of experience, they could not be empirical ones.

Readers are often inclined to think that Kant's identification of the categories has been too easily conducted. For him to speak of 'the clue' to their discovery leads one to expect more of a 'deduction' than we are offered, and the result seems to be that we are presented with little more than an arbitrary-looking list of concepts that carry very little individual weight. These suspicions are unjust. In the first place, the deduction of which Kant speaks here is only, and explicitly (B159), a deduction of the

a priori nature of the categories and has nothing to do with their identification. Indeed, as I have already indicated, the proposed deduction
can only be carried out once the identification has been achieved.

Then, in the Aesthetic the identification of Space and Time as the
forms of intuition required no argument, but only reflection, reflection
that they were ubiquitous throughout experience yet not given to us
within the manifold of sensibility. Similarly in the case of the categories.
Once we attend to the close connection between experience and judgement we see that the idea of something's being the case is a ubiquitous
feature of experience, and one that arises only through the various ways
in which the understanding combines the data of sense in the judgements
that it makes. Alert to the importance of judgement, then, and following
the 'guiding thread', our attention is easily enough led to the constant
presence of the categories in our experience. After that, simple reflection
of the kind just advanced should convince us of their *a priori* nature, just
as it did in the case of space and time.

What is left undiscussed is the completeness of the set of categories,
which is important for Kant just because the *Critique* aspires to identify
the totality of *a priori* knowledge we can come to concerning the nature
of experience. Again, we should not look for anything that might count
as a strict proof of completeness. All that Kant needs is the eye of a
taxonomist who takes care to overlook nothing in the surveyable forms
of judgement that we find ourselves making. Given that the guiding
thread directs the taxonomist's gaze in the right quarter, there need be
no fear of anything significant's going undetected. No more is really
needed to support the claim to completeness, and if, perchance, it should
turn out that something important has been overlooked, the oversight
may be expected to be easy to rectify.

It will be recalled that the concepts *space* and *time* were *necessary*
concepts as well as *a priori* ones, concepts on which our dependence on
sensibility obliges us to draw. In the very same sense of necessity, the
categories are necessary as well as being *a priori*, though this time it is our
dependence on understanding, not intuition, that ensures they permeate
our experience. It is they, and they alone, which connect the elements of
intuition in ways that represent something as being the case. In default of
that we would not have fully fledged experience at all. Thus, reflecting on
a purely hypothetical case, Kant observes that 'appearances might very
well be so constituted that the understanding should not find them to be
in accordance with the conditions of its unity' (A90/B123), only then he
points out that they would be nothing for us at all, merely something
'empty, null and meaningless'. So, if experience is to be capable of
providing us with knowledge, a state in which what is given in intuition

is indeed 'something for us', it cannot be understood except in terms of the categories.

Of course, it does not follow from this that each of the categories is singly necessary. All that has to be the case is that understanding should synthesize the passively given manifold in such a way as to represent this or that as being the case through the employment of some categories or other. However, Kant may well enough say that he is interested in what can be said about the *a priori* elements of the sort of experience that is ours, and not that of some imaginable intellectually less adventurous creatures than ourselves. For minded creatures to have the sort of experience of the world that we humans do, he can say, they must employ the whole range of *a priori* concepts that we dispose of. Unless they do that, the forms of judgement that they exercise will be diminished and the range of their experience consequently restricted.

That is all that needs to be said to secure the categories' necessity. However, at one point, at A112, Kant does envisage it as a general feature of their employment that they bind together the elements of intuition in ways that introduce necessity of a different sort. Thus, in thinking about the category of causality, he observes that we view the antecedent as necessitating the consequent, and he is tempted to generalize that thought to the other 'concepts of connection' that the categories are. What to make of this thought in the case of causation is something we shall come to in due course, but all that needs to be said about the implausibility of its extension to the other categories is that that will do nothing to impugn the sort of necessity just remarked on, and which they do enjoy. That is all that is needed to secure the identification of the categories as the necessary pure forms of understanding, just as similar reflection secured that status for Space and Time as the necessary pure forms of intuition.

My exposition of the Metaphysical Deduction has been conducted very much at arm's length from the text. That defect can be remedied by bringing it to bear on what I take to be the kernel of Kant's thought as that is expressed in the difficult sentences of A79/B104–5. There he writes: 'The same function which gives unity to the various representations *in a judgement* also gives unity to the mere synthesis of various representations *in an intuition*; and this unity...we entitle the pure concept of the understanding. The same understanding, through the same operations by which in concepts,...it produced the logical form of a judgement, also introduces a transcendental content into its representations...'

While these lines can hardly fail to make for bafflement on a first encounter, if my presentation of Kant's train of thought has been correct, they allow of reasonably straightforward paraphrase. Thus: what accounts for the ability of our judgements to combine their elements in ways that makes them assessible as true or false (= what 'gives unity to the various representations in a judgement') is the very same thing as provides our single experiences with their representational capacity (= the 'unity of various representations in an *intuition*'). Both sorts of unity must be due to the workings of some *a priori* concepts supplied in a completely formal way by the understanding. And as the understanding draws on these concepts in the production of complete judgements in one logical form or another, so it conceptualizes the manifold of experience in terms of them, thereby introducing a formal, *a priori* and transcendental content into the output of its synthesizing operation, that is, into the content of our experience itself.

It is notable that in this passage and, indeed, in the rest of this chapter of the Analytic of Concepts Kant does not say anything further about what the particular transcendental content is that is introduced into our synthesized intuitions by the operation of understanding. There is perhaps good enough reason for this in that it falls to the Analytic's next chapter, to the Transcendental Deduction, to be more explicit about that, and anything said here by way of detail could hardly avoid pre-empting that discussion. Nevertheless, from what has already been said it should be clear enough what this transcendental content is. It is that the operation of understanding as employed about the data of intuition obliges us to organize the manifold as a representation of *something's being the case*. This it achieves through the various ways in which it allows us to construct complete judgements. The content in question is 'transcendental' only in the technical sense of A11–12/B25 that this is how understanding has to combine the empirically given matter of sensibility if it is to operate at all, a condition on the very possibility of experience itself.

At this early stage, however, we have only a minimal understanding of what is involved in having experience as of something being the case, just as in the Metaphysical Exposition of the concepts *space* and *time* the mere information that those concepts were non-empirical yet necessary ones was itself minimally informative about what constraints those forms of intuition imposed on the sort of experience that we can have. And just as in the Aesthetic it fell to the Transcendental Exposition to develop the further consequences of the identification of the pure forms of intuition, so now just what follows from the recognition that our understanding has to operate to make sense of the data of intuition in terms of representations of this or that's being the case is also left to the fuller development of that idea in the immediately following Transcendental Deduction.

Before moving on, a last comment may be in order about Kant's speaking in this passage of the unity that the synthesis of representations has in an intuition, since it is far from obvious that our experience of the world must be thought of in terms of single items each with their particular unity. Indeed, as we have seen, the empiricist tradition found it quite natural to think of experience as a buzzing flow of sensation with no particular unity. So one might wonder whether Kant is not importing something quite gratuitously.

In passing, we have already noticed Kant's concession that there is logical space for intuition without thought (A90–1). And to the extent that anything is rightly conceived of as a mere buzzing flow of sensation that is how Kant would describe it. But, he would emphatically say, that is not yet anything 'for us'. As soon as we pause over elements of the intuitional flow and pick them out in one way or another and bring them under concepts in the form of judgements that record the ways in which they present themselves to us, we inevitably single them out as particular states of affairs which acquire a unity from the way in which we think of them. Independently of our bringing understanding to bear in that way they have no unity. Yet as soon as we focus our attention on this or that element of the manifold and bring understanding to bear on it in the form of judgement, so our experience presents us with particular states of affairs, intuitions that then have their unity precisely through the way in which judgement binds them together. In the next two chapters we shall see in greater detail how understanding, in making the flow of intuition 'something for us', brings with it notable constraints on what the world of appearance can be like.

4

Understanding, Objectivity and Self-consciousness: The Transcendental Deduction

The second chapter of the Analytic is the dense and perplexing 'Deduction of the Pure Concepts of Understanding'. Kant states the task before him as that of 'explaining the manner in which concepts [here, obviously, the categories, A.S.] can relate *a priori* to objects' (A85/B117), but that description is hardly clear enough to tell us what to expect. In fact, Kant has two distinct aims in view. The first is to convince the reader that the said concepts do not introduce distortion into our experience of the world by applying to it ideas that are ill adapted to it, as for example are the concepts *fate* and *fortune* (A84/B117). In that sense the 'deduction' seeks to show that the *a priori* concepts of the understanding have a legitimate application to what we experience. It is, as Kant explains, akin to a legal proof of title, a demonstration that one has a right to the enjoyment of a particular piece of property. And this 'deduction', or justification, is *transcendental* in that it will be completed by arguing that we cannot enjoy experience of the world except through application of the categories to the intuitional input with which we are passively supplied. They will be justified by a demonstration that it is only if the world is understood in their terms that it can be anything for us at all.

The second task Kant has in view is rather more reminiscent of the Transcendental Exposition of the Aesthetic, which, it will be remembered, is 'the explanation of a concept as a principle from which the possibility of other *a priori* synthetic knowledge can be understood' (A25/B40). Here, he adumbrates ways in which as we apply the categorial concepts to the manifold of intuition in making that something for us, that is, in experience, we necessarily represent the world as fully objective, as something distinct from our experiencing it, and furthermore as falling under laws that bind its various elements together, ultimately as a unified system of Nature. It is at this point that we see the full extent of Kant's Copernicanism, underpinned now by this ambitious reflection on the role played by understanding in the construction of experience. It is only through the use of understanding in this ample way that what is presented to us in sensibility becomes something for us. That can only happen through our combination of the manifold in judgement by means of the pure concepts of the understanding, and that in turn has to take place in accordance with these further demanding requirements. Once again, we see that the kind of system of Nature that we are bound to build up if we are to have any experience at all is a reflection of ourselves rather than of the world as it is in itself. In this way, Kant's Transcendental Idealism will be provided with support that is entirely new, and given a far richer positive content than it had received at the end of the earlier Aesthetic.

So much by way of broad outline. The difficulty is to see exactly what these conclusions amount to, and just how they are meant to be reached. Kant himself advertised the extreme difficulty of the task at A98 and, in the hope of reducing the obscurity of his first attempt on it, rewrote all but the introductory section of the Deduction for the *Critique*'s second edition. Regrettably though, that exercise did not make the reader's work all that much easier. In my own presentation of this part of the argument I shall draw principally on the B version, albeit making free use of its predecessor as and when seems helpful. I shall also be guided more by what Kant wanted to achieve than by the detail of the procedure he adopted to that end in his text.

Although we saw the Metaphysical Deduction claiming that our reliance on understanding introduces transcendental content into experience, it neither explicitly identified that content, nor did it suggest that what is so introduced might not in some way radically distort our grasp of the world and cause us to represent it in falsifying ways. While I suggested that it is plain what that content is, to wit, that through understanding one arrives at experience that represents something *as being the case*, it should be acknowledged that that is not an expression that Kant himself uses. Nor does he there even suggest that there is any one such common content introduced into our experience by whatever particular categories on which we happen to draw as we synthesize the manifold of intuition from time to time.

However, in the preliminary passage of the Transcendental Deduction that is common to both editions, Kant is somewhat more forthcoming, saying: 'Now all experience does contain, in addition to the intuition of the senses through which something is given, a *concept* of an object as being thereby given, that is to say, as appearing' (A93/B126), and it is plain enough from the context that this 'concept of an object being given' is precisely what comes with the understanding's employment of the categories. I take it again as clear enough from the context that the term 'object given' here is not to be understood as some individual item we encounter in our experience, a fox-terrier, say, or a billiard ball or a table-lamp. Rather it must be understood as anything that we experience as being thus and so, and which I spoke of above just as something or other's being the case, or as a state of affairs. It is that 'relation to an object' that Kant explicitly holds to be introduced through judgement in general, thus confirming the identification of the 'transcendental content' introduced in the earlier discussion of the categories.[1]

Given that this is the fundamental idea that supposedly comes with judgement itself and which is articulated in different ways through the 12 pure categorial concepts that the understanding disposes of as it goes about its synthesizing business, there is a swift enough route to the assurance Kant wants that the categories are not mere 'wind-bubbles' or 'usurpatory concepts' like those of *fortune* and *fate*. This is that the 'concept of an object', or that of something's being the case, is precisely the idea of the objective validity of experience.[2] And while many of our judgements as of something's being the case may in fact not be true, it cannot possibly be the case that that idea has no application at all. For the idea of a concept's having no application is the same as nothing answering to the concept within the range of possible representations of the world, as is the case with the concepts *fate, fortune, phlogiston, unicorn* and the like. The idea of something's being the case, by contrast, could not be like that since the whole range of our experience consists in representations as of something's being the case. It is only within that range that it makes sense to ask whether a concept has application or not. Since the categorial concepts function to establish that feature of our experience, they themselves provide the framework with respect to which we ask of a given concept whether or not it has application. They themselves could not possibly fail to do so. As Kant puts it, the categories 'relate of necessity and *a priori* to objects of experience, for the reason that only by means of them can any object whatever of experience be thought' (A93/B126).

In the A version of the deduction the same idea is expressed a little more clearly:

The *a priori* conditions of a possible experience in general are at the same time conditions of the possibility of objects of experience. Now I maintain that the categories, above cited, are nothing but the conditions of thought in a possible experience, just as space and time are the conditions of intuition for that same experience. They are fundamental concepts by which we think objects in general for appearances, and have therefore *a priori* objective validity. This is exactly what we desired to prove. (A111)

There is something that needs to be remarked on here and borne in mind for future discussion. If the idea of objective validity that comes with Kant's 'concept of an object' is merely that we order our experiences by representing something as being the case, the thought that that idea cannot fail to have application cannot exactly be the thought that some of our experiential representations must actually be true or correct. Rather it is that experience couldn't fail to represent something as being thus and so, whether or not those judgements ultimately turn out to be true. The idea of objective validity pervades one's experience. So, even though at A125, in a bracket and without any further remark, Kant does gloss the idea of objective validity as that of truth, that can only mean that putting forward things as being true under the truth-directed investigative and critical guidance of understanding is what pervades our experience. Seen like that, even judgements that pass muster by the evidential standards of sound judgement, but which in fact are false, can pretend to objective validity. Consequently, endorsing Kant's thought that the categories are not usurpatory concepts is quite distinct from asserting in transcendental fashion that many, or even any, of the experiential judgements that we make in using them must be true. If there is an argument for that, it must lie elsewhere. The same thing will hold of whatever further content comes to be attached to 'the concept of an object' as Kant develops that.[3]

Let us suppose then that the first of Kant's two aims is fulfilled in this way. It none the less remains true that the idea of what it is to an object of experience or what it is for our judgements to be objectively valid is quite minimally understood. It is plain from the text that Kant believes that there is something substantial to be said here and something which is quite unlike the provision of a general criterion for the truth of our judgements or the accuracy of our experience, which he rightly recognizes to be out of the question.[4] At this point it will be helpful to move in two stages. First we can pick out how Kant takes the idea of objectivity to be manifested in experience; and then we can look at the reasons he offers for thinking it an *a priori* matter that, for minds like ours, it should be manifested in just that way.

The first substantial descriptive claim is that objects of experience are distinct from our representations of them. They are 'whatever corresponds to, and must consequently be distinct from, our knowledge' (A104). Secondly, what it is in our synthesizing of the elements of experience that allows us to introduce such distinct things into appearance is that we deploy our understanding in ways that are not 'arbitrary and haphazard' (A104 again). This inevitably comes with seeing the various elements of our representations as being *connected in the objects* or states of affairs themselves, and not simply as reflecting the way in which we are affected by them in the flow of our perceptions. We can say that for Kant it will follow from this that as we exercise understanding in making sense of what is given to us in intuition, and take it that we are aware of this or that as being the case, so we synthesize the manifold in ways that have definite implications for the behaviour the represented objects will display under various hypothetical conditions.

To give an example, making sense of what is now in front of my eyes as a computer keyboard placed on the desk before me, I know such things as that the effect of pressing the keys will not remove it from my line of vision; that if I turn it upside down it will not present the same set of keys to view; that if I unplug it, the screen will be unaffected by my continuing to type, and so on. Unless these conditionals hold and many another like them, I shall have to retract my attempt to deploy my conceptualizing understanding in that particular 'keyboard' way. It would not then have achieved that experiential 'relation to an object' that its synthesizing aims at. As Kant puts it: 'In so far as our modes of knowledge are to relate to an object, they must necessarily agree with one another, that is, must possess that unity which constitutes the concept of an object' (A104–5), and that will apply as much to the broad conception of 'object' as *state of affairs* that I have recommended as to any narrower one that might be preferred.

A further element built into Kant's conception of objectivity or objective validity, though not one that is very much to the fore in this part of the *Critique*, is the idea of publicity (see in particular the much later passage at A820/B848). Kant considers the example of my judging a body to be heavy. I make that judgement on the basis of feeling myself lift it and then having an impression of weight. My judgement that the body is heavy does not merely state that the representations are conjoined in my own perception, but that they are combined *in the object* (B141–2), and a little earlier on (B140) that sort of unity is said to be 'necessarily and universally valid'. Just what that signifies is none too clear from the context, but Kant's own teachers' guide to the *Critique*, the *Prolegomena to Any Future Metaphysics as a Science* (1783), makes plain that what he has in mind is that necessarily, if a judgement I make enjoys objective validity, anyone placed as I am will concur with me on pain of being mistaken.[5] This, of course, is just what we should expect, since Kant takes it that we all have our situation within the one space-and-time that there is, and that that could be the way the world is given to us in intuition only if our representing it in terms of states of affairs holding entailed its presenting itself in the very same ways to any true judges who do, or might, view it from the same position at the same time.

These scant descriptive thoughts of Kant's appear in the course of his brief elucidation of 'our concept of an *object in* general'. In the A edition they also serve to introduce the opaque idea of the 'transcendental object = x', something that entirely disappears from the B version of the Deduction. A short digressive comment about this should be all that is needed. In the 1781 edition Kant thinks that what is immediately given to us in perception are appearances, which he finds hard to distinguish clearly from the things that are represented in those appearances. At the same time he is insistent that appearances need to be appearances of something, and for him that means more than that they just have intentional content. Yet we already know from the Aesthetic that the objects of experience that we come to synthesize from the manifold are not and cannot be things-in-themselves. They have therefore to be something else. So he writes: 'The pure concept of this transcendental object, which in reality throughout all our knowledge is always one and the same, is what can alone confer upon all our empirical concepts in general relation to an object, that is, objective reality. This concept cannot contain any determinate intuition, and therefore refers only to that unity which must be met with in any manifold of knowledge which stands in relation to an object' (A109).[6]

Elsewhere in the *Critique* the expressions 'transcendental object' and 'transcendental subject' do unequivocally refer to elements of the world as it is in itself, the noumenal world, as e.g. at A191/B236. Here, however, such a reading may well not make best sense.[7] What appears to make rather better sense in this context is to see the 'transcendental object' as designating the form experience has to take as the synthesizing activity of the understanding imbues it with objective validity. Thus, as we have just seen, what appears in our experience is thought of as of something distinct from our representations themselves, something public and orderly. This requirement is the same in all cases, and that would be why the transcendental object is 'always one and the same throughout all our knowledge'. It is introduced somewhat algebraically as '$= x$' on this view just because it is thought of only as 'something in general' (A104), something that is a constant form that any object of experience shares with any other. Once this is understood, and once it is understood that the idea introduces nothing beyond what comes with the categories themselves and the transcendental content that they introduce into experience, puzzlement evaporates. As far as Kant's exposition goes, the 'transcendental object' is strictly speaking redundant on this reading. That would be enough to explain its absence from the Deduction in the B edition.[8]

The final element in Kant's idea of 'object of experience' is an ambitious extension of the idea that understanding cannot combine our representations in ways that are utterly haphazard and arbitrary. This is that they should 'fit into a connected whole of human knowledge' (A121), and ultimately that what is presented to us in experience should make up a system of Nature, one that is through and through governed by natural law (A125–7/B163–5). As we synthesize our perceptual data in terms of states of affairs distinct from our perception of them, we do so in terms of ways in which they interact with other such states of affairs, and at the purely descriptive level we may think that there is going to be no upper bound to the range of conditional judgements that we may want to make that bear on the objectivity of the claims we put forward. (Unless unplugged, the keyboard I see will cause me agony if I drop it into my bath; it will shatter if thrown hard at the wall; it will not be eaten by the hungry dogs, etc.) This extension of the earlier idea of orderliness in experience is what leads Kant to say dramatically that '[h]owever exaggerated and absurd it may sound, to say that the understanding is itself the source of the laws of nature, and so of its formal unity, such an assertion is nonetheless correct, and is in keeping with the object to which it refers, namely, experience' (A127).

The challenge that the reader faces is to make out how Kant proposes to secure these various, so far purely descriptive, claims about the character of our experience as genuinely transcendental conditions on the very nature of experience itself, conditions that are brought by the understanding into the ways we synthesize our intuitions, and not just as a contingent reflection of the world in which we live. Certainly, Kant readily asserts that '[c]ategories are concepts which prescribe laws *a priori to* appearances, and therefore to nature, the sum of appearances' (B163), yet one could be forgiven for thinking that there is a very wide gap indeed between modestly judging something to be the case, which is the most the metaphysical deduction identified as the function of the categories, and these more audacious ideas that doing that is said to bring with it in *a priori* fashion.

To this protest Kant will reply that mooted gap only appears to yawn; it does not really do so. For no mention has yet been made of the idea that is so central to both versions of the Deduction – rather more firmly in place in B than in A – and which goes under the title of the 'transcendental unity of apperception'. This, Kant announces, is 'the first principle of human understanding' (B139), and the necessity of its holding is ultimately what ensures that the richly conceived idea of objectivity reigns in our experience rather than any more modest one that might initially be supposed adequate to fill out the unassuming notion of this or that's being the case.

In this chapter and the last, and following Kant's usage, I have repeatedly spoken of understanding making its objects something *for me*. This is effectively nothing other than for me to be self-consciously aware of something as this or that, or to judge it in such a way as I can say to myself 'I think that *p*' or 'it is to me as if *p*'. And Kant takes it that this self-conscious capability is analytically connected with the deployment of the understanding in its synthesis of experience (B138), so that we must be able to think of any experience that we have that it is ours or that that is how things are for us. 'Apperception' is the traditional term for such self-conscious awareness, and in using it Kant is doing no more than drawing on its well-established significance.[9]

Kant makes it plain that while the manifold is given to us over time, what the understanding has to do is to bring together our various apprehensions under concepts which link what is given at different times in one *single* self-consciousness. This singularity is the *unity* of apperception. By way of contrast, consider that I might apprehend some element of the manifold as mine at one moment and a different element as mine at another, only just by itself that would not yet involve any *unity* of self-consciousness. Even though both are apperceived, and not merely perceived, the two incidents might be as unconnected for me as are the self-conscious experiences of Potiphar and of Potiphar's wife. For my apperception to enjoy unity, I have to be aware of both elements *as* given to one and the same persisting self, and that Kant thinks is something that must hold of any experience that individual subjects of experience can come to have. We could put it by saying that any experience I have has to be of a kind that allows me to attribute it to the very same self as any other experience that I happen to have. Experience on the basis of which I can think of myself as an 'abiding and unchanging "I" ', is, Kant says, what 'forms the correlate of all our representations in so far as it is to be at all possible that we should become conscious of them' (A123). A little earlier on much the same point is made by his saying: 'All possible appearances, as representations, belong to the totality of a possible self-consciousness. But as self-consciousness is a transcendental representation, numerical identity is inseparable from it' (A113).

As so often, Kant is less than forthcoming with argument to support a pivotal thought, and clearly this one needs refinement if it is to accommodate experiences we have which slip from consciousness as time passes, as when we are beset by memory failure, or of which we are unconscious, or which we somehow repress, for while such experiences are indeed mine (that is, they belong to the person who denies having had them) that is not enough for Kant's condition to be met. They are not self-consciously mine, not apperceptively united. Kant's way of dealing with the difficulty is to say that the unity of apperception is best expressed hypothetically and not categorically, so that even if not all my experiences are actually apperceptively united, they all could be. Thus: 'As *my* representations (even if I am not conscious of them as such) they must conform to the condition under which alone they *can* stand together in one universal self-consciousness, because otherwise they would not all belong to me' (B132). In these passages Kant shies away from explaining what makes it possible for different representations to be united in one self-consciousness when in fact they are not. In particular, he does not take the route of saying that they could only belong to one consciousness in so far as they are experiences of the same embodied subject, which is a possibility that I explore on his behalf in chapter 6 below. However, the detail is something that need not perhaps be pursued too keenly here, since all that is important for now is, (a), that we do all think of ourselves as persisting subjects of self-conscious experience and, (b), that the central claim of the transcendental deduction is that this fixed truth about ourselves carries with it implications about the way in which we are bound to deploy the categories in making sense of the manifold that comes our way in intuition.

The way Kant's mind moves in A is to see this condition of numerical identity being satisfied only as our various representations are united in the objects of our experience. They need to enjoy what he calls *affinity* rather than mere *association* (A112–13). In B, he puts it by saying that the necessary unity of apperception reveals the necessity of a synthesis of the manifold given in intuition (B135), and this synthesis is nothing other than bringing the various representations given to me in intuition together in the concept of an object, understood now in the rich way earlier described.

So I take it that the train of thought Kant is pursuing at this point in the argument is that while it might look to be no more than a contingency that the kind of world we find experience revealing to us is one that is of states of affairs distinct from our apprehension of them, one that is orderly, public and in a large measure inductively tractable (or, as Kant would have it, governed by laws), in fact when we appreciate that our experience is necessarily bound together as that of one persisting self-conscious subject, we see that experience cannot but take on that familiar character. The necessity of this kind of operation of the understanding,

Kant will say, is 'the first pure knowledge of understanding' (B137). In the absence of such synthesis 'the manifold would *not be* united in one consciousness' (B138).

Naturally enough, one would like these far-reaching claims to be backed by substantive argument, yet however carefully one trawls the Deduction the net comes up pretty empty. Equally naturally, it is tempting to spend time and effort asking what Kant might have offered to support what in my presentation must seem to be exciting and grandiose claims. But perhaps both disappointment and attempts at dike-stopping are premature, for it is extremely difficult to see what resources are available to Kant to buttress or fill out our idea of objectivity independently of discussion of the way in which understanding operates in synthesizing the manifold within the forms of space and time. Since the discussion of the Deduction has kept that aspect of things very much in the background – and indeed in the B version has postponed towards its very end all insistence that the objectivity of our experience can only arise as understanding is brought to bear on the representations given in intuition – it may be better to look to Kant for support at this sensitive point only as that further material comes to the fore, as it does in the immediately following chapters of the Analytic. That, anyway, is the strategy I propose to pursue.

What is left over for the present discussion is to establish the connection between the handling of understanding in the Deduction and Transcendental Idealism. Earlier on, I said it is helpful to treat the Analytic as running largely parallel to the Aesthetic, and since the Aesthetic purported to be able to introduce Kantian idealism by reflection on intuition without allusion to understanding, we may suppose that at the end of the Deduction we shall find the same idealism emerging from consideration of understanding in abstraction from any thought about intuition. There is a way in which this expectation is fulfilled; there is also a way in which it is disappointed.

First, what is the claim we have to consider? It is that our experience as of a world of nature constituting a connected whole of human knowledge that systematically falls under natural laws cannot rightly be taken to be experience of the world as it is in itself. Since this broad claim derives from the necessary objective validity of our experience, and that derives directly from our use of pure concepts of the understanding in judgement, we have a clear parallel with the way Kant thinks about the spatiality and temporality of intuition. This parallel is reinforced by the way in which, just as the concepts of space and time cannot be derived from any manifold that is empirically given in intuition, at B163 Kant reminds us that the categories 'determine *a priori* the combination of the manifold of nature, while yet they are not derived from it'. So nature's lawlikeness has to be accounted for, just as its spatio-temporality, by reference to the fixed nature and structure of our minds.

We saw before that Kant took the *a priori* nature of the concepts *space* and *time* to legitimate the claim that intuition could only be of the world as it appears and not of the world as it is in itself. That doctrine looked insecure as long as it was left open whether things in themselves might not also be spatio-temporally organized, whether or not our concepts of space and time were empirically acquired. In chapter 2 above I suggested that Kant has an argument ready to hand to provide the needed support. As we turn to the idea of nature's being governed by law, however, the same strategy appears not to be available, for at B164 Kant explicitly says that 'Things in themselves would necessarily, apart from any understanding that knows them, conform to laws of their own.' So, one may wonder whether at this point the parallel between intuition and understanding is not breaking down. To that query there are at least two different responses to consider.

The first is that Kant makes it quite plain that the categories have no other content than a purely formal one so long as they are not exercised about material supplied in intuition. This is just a special application of the dictum of A51/B75 that 'thoughts without content are empty, intuitions without concepts are blind'. However, so long as the pure concepts are brought to bear on the deliverances of intuition, be that sensible intuition of the kind ours is or quite a different one, should there, or could there, be such, they will inevitably import a kind of transcendental content into the experiences of such intuition's subjects.[10] Bearing in mind that Kant believes that judging itself, the bringing of various representations (intuitions) under other representations (concepts) itself makes it necessary to synthesize the manifold in accordance with the unity of apperception, he would presumably say the same of experiential judgements based on others' intuition as he says about the judgements that we humans are able to make. So, the features of distinctness, publicity, orderliness and the law-governed nature of the world are going to be attributed to the world as it appears not just to the human mind, but also as it appears to any minds whose intuitional and passively received data are significantly unlike our own.

However, despite this notable element of community between the human and the non-human conception of objects of experience, it would be moving too quickly to suppose that this might ultimately be accounted for by the world in itself enjoying that same character. We have to keep constantly in mind that these rich features of Kantian objectivity derive from the ways in which we or others make judgements about the world of appearance in consonance with the unity of apperception. It is not that whatever lends itself to such judgement must possess that character; rather these ideas apply to what is experienced only as it comes to be judged or synthesized. Given this peculiarly Kantian take on things, just because the world in itself is presumed to be fully determined independently of being judged by subjects of one kind or another, it is bound to resist any such characterization. That is the first response to our question and one that firmly maintains the putative parallel between the Aesthetic and the Analytic.

This speculative reading of Kant's position is nowhere explicitly endorsed in the text, and appears to run flatly counter to the assertion of B164, noted a couple of paragraphs back. Anyone who is determined to maintain the parallel between Aesthetic and Analytic will probably regard this as a stray eccentric observation, and, moreover, one that going by his own reckoning, Kant has no business to make. However, if instead we take that pronouncement *au pied de la lettre* a different response is prompted to the original question. It is to say that no experience we or others might have could be of a kind to give us *knowledge* of the world's objectivity unless we take that objectivity to be restricted to the world as it appears. The reason is that, as we have seen, the objectively experienced world must fall under laws, which are from Kant's point of view rules that are necessary (A113, 126). The necessity of the rules is hardly anything other than their strict and exceptionless universality, and I have suggested that what allows them to enjoy that status in our experience is the spontaneity of our understanding, which we are able to exercise simply by refusing to accept apparent breakdowns in regularities as genuine breakdowns. Their necessity is thus *a priori* just because it is ultimately a matter for us and not the world itself to uphold our determination to treat them in that way. If now we suppose our experience of the world to be not just of the world as it appears but of it as it is in itself, we could not know that the regularities in it that we encounter are instances of laws just because we could not know them to be strictly universal even if that is what they were. So, given that the objectivity of experience brings with it the synthesis of intuition in ways that display genuine lawlikeness, it could only be fit to give us knowledge of the world of appearance whether or not the world in itself is also governed by law.[11/12]

In this discussion of the Deduction, the concluding chapter of the Analytic of Concepts, I have where possible, and following Kant, focused on the understanding independently of the way in which it interacts with intuition. That is the topic immediately following Analytic of Principles, to which we shall shortly turn. However, at the end of the Deduction's

B version, Kant completes his proof of the universal application of the categories by insisting that to the extent that we find a unity in intuitive, sensible experience – say as presenting us with a conjunction of things in space and time – that too must be attributed to the categories. So, *whatever* unity experience manifests, be it in judgement or in the intuitively given manifold, is subject to the categories (B144–5, B160–1, and footnotes). At that point Kant feels he can say that 'by demonstration of the *a priori* validity of the categories in respect of all objects of our senses the purpose of the deduction will be fully attained' (B145).

It may well seem at first that Kant does not need to labour the point, since if 'thoughts without content are empty', one could well find oneself saying that they get their content from sensible intuition, and that as they do so intuition will be subject to the categories. But that reflection does not take Kant quite as far as he wants to go. For his idea is not just that the categories apply to intuition as that is brought to judgement, but that intuitions can *only* get their unity from judgement, and that to suppose otherwise, as we might if we reflect on the seeming spatial and temporal unity of our surroundings in what appears to be unthinking experience, is a kind of illusion. We have to understand that unity as a spontaneous combinatorial action of our thought about what is given to us in sensibility. Resulting from spontaneous acts of synthesis, it is necessarily arrived at through the application of the categories to the data of sense, whether we are aware of that happening or not (B152).

Kant's conclusion, then, is that wherever there is unity in our experience it is attributable to the synthesis of the understanding, and since experience is not possible without the combination of sensible elements, all experience proper is subject to the categories. What then of the earlier thought that experience might in certain circumstances turn out to be chaotic?

> Appearances might very well be so constituted that the understanding should not find them in accordance with the conditions of its unity. Everything might be in such confusion that, for instance, in the series of appearances nothing presented itself which might yield a rule of synthesis and so answer to the concept of cause and effect. This concept would then be altogether empty, null and meaningless. But since intuition stands in no need whatsoever of the functions of thought, appearances would none the less present objects to our intuition. (A90/B123)

Setting aside the occurrence of the word 'objects' (*Gegenstände*) at the end of these sentences, it should now be clear what Kant's considered position is. Such chaos could not be the presentation of something as being the case, would not be something for me, but precisely a situation in which I could make nothing of what sensibility offers. It would not be a case of the categories failing to apply to the world, since in such turmoil the world would not be given to me at all. What then of those '*objects present to out intuition*'? The answer must be that they could be no more than the buzzing sensations of which I can make nothing. It is not just the concepts of cause and effect which have no sense there, are empty, null and meaningless. No concept has any application for me, not even the concept *chaos*, even if what assails me in the situation is chaos itself.

The Deduction is now complete. The initially exiguous idea of object-ive validity imported into experience by the spontaneity of the under-standing has given way to a descriptively far fuller one. That, in turn, is held in place transcendentally by the necessity of the unity of appercep-tion that governs any experience we might come to have. So, of necessity, the categories govern any experience we might have of the world, and they have to do so in the ample way that has been set out. In addition, Kant has claimed that objectively valid experience may amount to know-ledge, but that when it does, the sort of objectivity that our knowledge enjoys must, as far as its formal aspects go, reflect the nature of our minds, not that of the world as it is in itself.

While Kant writes in tones that suggest he believes he has provided convincing arguments for these claims, going by the philosophical stand-ards of a later age it has to be said that everything that turns on the introduction of the unity of apperception cries out for further support than the Deduction provides. Perhaps Kant himself had a good sense of this, since a fair amount of the immediately following Analytic of Prin-ciples can be readily harnessed to this task.

5

The Principles of Pure Understanding

Considered on their own and without any relation to intuition, the categories are purely formal concepts (A139/B178). It is Kant's view that the specific content they come to display as they are applied to what is given in intuition is partially determined by the forms of intuition themselves. Restrictions on the categories that arise from the interplay of the forms of intuition and the forms of understanding in their empirical cooperation generate the most notable range of *a priori* knowledge we can have about the world that we are given to experience. Not only do the categories themselves acquire a particular character as they are employed about our intuition, but in addition, each of the four groups of categories, those of quantity, quality, relation and modality, generate determinate Principles that fix how what is presented to us in space and time must be if our experience is to enjoy the objectivity that the Transcendental Deduction has identified as internal to it. Since for us humans that is how any world has to be presented, at this crucial juncture of the *Critique* we again find Kant's thought attaining a notable transcendental dimension.

In one way we have already seen the content that the categories import into experience being constrained by something other then themselves. It was the necessity of those concepts being subject to the unity of apperception that gave Kant's notion of objectivity the great richness that it achieved in the Deduction. Now we find other restrictions on their deployment in our empirical experience deriving from the further requirement that it has always to conform to the form of inner sense, time. This is the theme of the brief first chapter of the Analytic of Principles, to which Kant gave the title 'The Schematism of the Pure Concepts of the Understanding'.

The leading idea of the Schematism is simple enough and need not hold us up for long. Nevertheless, it will be as well to spend a brief moment with it since it provides a helpful way of approaching the much fuller Principles that occupy the following sections of the Analytic. Kant starts off from the thought that it is a condition of our empirical concepts having a significant use that they enjoy a certain homogeneity with the objects that fall under them. He instances the concept *round*, and says that we could have a use for it only if it were in its way akin to things which are given to us in intuition, such as plates. The idea is not promising, since it can ultimately come to little more than the thought that concepts have a meaningful use for us only if associated with determinate truth conditions or assertibility conditions, and put like that the idea of homogeneity that Kant pins his discussion on simply evaporates. It may well be that what we have here is merely a residue of the earlier widespread idea that concepts are the same as ideas, and ideas fit the world as they resemble it (cf., for example, Locke on primary qualities (*Essay* II.viii.15), or Descartes on the innateness of even our empirical ideas (*Comments on a Certain Broadsheet*)). At any rate, it would be unwise to try to make the notion of homogeneity bear great weight in understanding what Kant is about.

Be this as it may, drawing on this dubious thought Kant points out that there is nothing in the intuitive data of experience to which the pure categorial concepts answer (*scilicet*, resemble), and that might suggest that they could have no place in experience, failing the homogeneity requirement as they do. Yet how could that be, since the Deduction has shown that they must absolutely pervade it? Kant's response to the apparent difficulty is to claim that as we bring understanding to bear on the manifold of intuition, just because the judgements we make are about what is given to us in time, the categories come to be temporalized, or 'schematized', in one way or another, and being thus schematized acquire sufficient 'homogeneity' to lend themselves to significant empirical employment. Hence, just as understanding has to bring the categories to bear in its synthesis of the manifold, so it is obliged to do so through their schemata, and the content which that move brings with it cannot but determine the fundamental nature of our experience. A couple of examples illustrate the gist of Kant's thought.

Suppose I have a visual experience as of a red ball. The judgement implicit in that experience of mine may be 'That ball is red.' The form of the judgement being assertoric and categorical means that my experience is governed by the categorial concept *inherence and subsistence*. That purely formal notion does not directly match anything given to me in my experience, but as employed about what is given in time enables me to conceptualize my manifold in terms of a persisting substance (the ball). Unlike the formal concept of inherence and subsistence (being a subject of predication), that of substance, or of something real that persists through time, is eminently realizable in empirical terms, in this particular case in the guise of that red ball. The upshot is that we see how the categorical judgement in terms of which understanding orders the manifold draws on its essential formal concepts in a meaningful way. We are also led to recognize that in this particular case the notion of persisting substance is a legitimate and unavoidable one, even though it has to be accounted non-empirical and *a priori*.

Another example: I catch you with the ball in your hand eyeing a tempting window. I see you as being about to break the window by hurling the ball at it. My experience of you embodies a hypothetical judgement – if you throw the ball, you will break the window – employing the category of conditional dependence (textually, *Causality and Dependence* (A80/B106)). In its pure unschematized form the concept matches nothing in the experience I have, but schematized in terms of a temporal succession of events subject to a rule (cause and effect) (A144/B183), it serves very well. Just as before, we have a pointer to how, despite the lack of homogeneity, through their schemata the categorial concepts find a substantive place in our experience, and insight into how the idea of lawlike causation which is so pervasive there comes to make a transcendental and *a priori* contribution to it.

The Schematism then tells us something about the way in which the necessary temporality of our experience makes its impact on the experiential content that the categories come to have (A148/B188). After more or less simply outlining the schemata of the various categories one by one (A142–5/B182–4), Kant passes on in his next chapter to consider various Principles that he takes these inevitable restrictions on the categories' use to force onto our construction of the world. In effect, the Principles of Pure Understanding all provide answers of one sort or another to the question: What can we say by way of synthetic *a priori* truths about the nature of the world we experience? The quite general answer that emerges at the end of the Principles is a very striking one: our dependence on understanding the world in terms of the schematized categories is what guarantees it to be amenable to scientific investigation. This is striking because, with this in hand, Kant can claim to have carried through Descartes' own ambitious, yet philosophically flawed, attempt to revolutionize our understanding of the natural world through replacing the then going Aristotelian, hylomorphic, account of it by a fully mechanistic one.[1]

Before considering any specific Principles, Kant considers the matter in general and entirely abstract terms. There is a Highest Principle of analytic judgement, and so presumably a Highest Principle of synthetic judgement too. The former is the Principle of Non-Contradiction, and need not detain us. The latter is derived from the Deduction, and is the principle that transcendental conditions on the possibility of experience are at the same time necessary conditions on the objects of experience. So if it is necessary that my intuitional awareness of something or some state of affairs should abide by certain conditions, it must be the case that what I thereby experience itself abide by those conditions. What underlies Kant's thought here is the idea that unless this Principle held we would find that objects of experience could not be given to us. And since they are and can only be given to us through our intuitions, if those intuitions are constrained by conditions XYZ, the objects that thereby appear to us will themselves have to be synthesized as being XYZ (A155–7/B194–6).

The first of the Principles that Kant discusses, the Axioms of Intuition (A162–6/B202–7), illustrates this general thought and provides us with what Kant holds to be a great enlargement of our *a priori* knowledge. This is that the axioms and theorems of mathematics (specifically those of Euclidean geometry and elementary arithmetic) do not merely have their ground in the formal character of the intuitions or apprehensions whereby we experience the world, but more than that necessarily apply to the world of objects that is constructed from those intuitions. This is of the greatest significance, just because without that assurance the Cartesian conception of a fully mathematizable and measurable world would be no more than a matter of blind, unwarranted faith. In this way it can be said that the Principles start to lay down for Kant the metaphysical foundations of natural science.

The argument Kant relies on to secure his conclusion is two-fold. In its geometrical formulation, it sets off from the thought that as we synthesize objects out of what is given to us in spatial intuition, we are obliged to construct the wholes out of parts; we can do no other than build up apprehensions of the wholes from apprehensions of their single elements (A163/B204). This, Kant supposes, is what enables us to view them as extensive magnitudes. And it is only because the wholes are constructed in apprehension out of intuitions of parts that we can say that between two points only one straight line is possible and the like. Were that constructive story not to hold, there is no way in which we should have reason to think any such thing; we should just not be able to experience any such figure. And since this is a transcendental condition on our intuition of objects, it will follow by the Highest Principle of synthetic judgement that the objects constructively synthesized from our intuitions must themselves also be extensive magnitudes that conform to the axioms of (Euclidean) geometry.

Likewise, we may presume, when it comes to the theorems of arithmetic. Because the number series must be constructed from the way in which our apprehensions succeed one another in time – the series being constructed by counting off successive experiential moments (A142–3/ B182) – so the objects that we experience must also lend themselves to numerical quantification. Just as the spatial form governing our apprehensions (the *a priori* form of outer sense) generates the geometrical nature of the world that we synthesize from them, so the necessarily temporal nature of our intuitions ensures the applicability of arithmetical thought to the reality we construct on their basis.[2]

So at once a double step in the Cartesian programme is taken: necessarily the objects of experience that we construct through the synthesis of intuition are themselves geometrically and arithmetically mathematizable. However, this gain in our intellectual grasp of the world does come, for Kant, at a cost Descartes would have been loath to pay. It is that the ambition of mathematizing the world can only be fulfilled if, Descartes to the contrary, the world is not taken to be the world in itself. Taken like that, we could say no more than that it would at best be a contingency that the world's objects possess magnitude, and even if it were we should have no assurance that they would continue to do so in the future.[3] Restricting ourselves to the world of appearance, though, not only do we see what underlies its mathematizability, but we also see that it is necessarily mathematizable (A165–6/B206–7). So interpreted, Cartesianly inspired science is at no risk from the future.

A second Principle, likewise constitutive of intuitive experience, derives from the categories of quality and goes under the name of 'Anticipations of Perception' (A166–76/B207–18). It is manifest this time not in consideration of the successive nature of our synthesizing of appearances, but of the momentary nature of our single intuitive apprehensions. The principle in question is that no matter what its content, at any moment our awareness of things must enjoy some positive degree of intensity. For example, momentary sensitivity to temperature will have to be of some degree of heat, to weight, some moment of gravity, to colour, some positive degree of hue, and so on. From this, together with the same Highest Principle, Kant infers as before that appearances (= objects of perception) themselves must possess a degree of influence on the senses (which he calls an intensive magnitude) (A166/B208). From this he concludes in *a priori* fashion that all reality must be marked by continuity, intensive as well as extensive (A170/B212). Not only can there never be a true vacuum, for that could never be given in appearance, but also we see that it is an *a priori* truth that it must be mistaken to explain the difference of weight, say, between bodies of equal volume by appeal to one being emptier than the other. The intensive magnitude in the object which accounts for its registering so much weight can diminish *ad infinitum* without leaving any part of the space occupied by the body truly empty (A174/B216).[4]

Kant thinks of the Axioms of Intuition and Anticipations of Perception as constitutive of any appearance whatever, and as deriving directly from their necessary application to what is given in intuition and from the formal requirements that that imposes on the understanding as it conceptualizes the manifold in line with the schematized categories. Because they serve to secure the amenability of reality to different sorts of measurement, extensive and intensive, it is natural for him to speak of them as *mathematical* principles. Important though they are for Kant's overall project of grounding natural science, they have generally attracted less commentary than the immediately succeeding Analogies of Experience. By contrast, these and the following Postulates of Empirical Thought are not principles that are constitutive of single intuitions or apprehensions so much as regulative of the way in which our different intuitions are to be connected with one another in the construction of the world of appearance, not mathematical but, as Kant puts it, *dynamical*.[5] Despite this difference, though, these dynamical principles still express synthetic *a priori* truths about the world of appearance itself and are constitutive of it no less than their mathematical counterparts (A664/B692).

The overall concern of the Analogies (A176–218/B218–65) is how understanding has to operate if the world of our experience is to be fully temporal. The approach Kant takes is by confronting the issue of how we structure the objective world out of the flow of apprehensions. As we saw earlier on, the manifold of intuition, the flow of sensory impressions, takes place in time, but does not contain within itself any temporal content. That was fundamentally why our possession of the gamut of temporal (and spatial) concepts could not be empirical ones, and so had to be *a priori*. Given that an objective world has to be constructed under the categorial concepts, it must be by their means that the world of experience acquires its obligatory temporal dimension. As Kant puts it at A177, stating the general principle of the Analogies, 'All appearances [that is, things that appear, A.S.] are, as regards their existence, subject *a priori* to rules determining their relation to one another in time', a sentence that gets replaced in the B edition by 'Experience [viz., of objects, states of affairs, A.S.] is possible only through the representation of a necessary connection of perceptions' (B218). Recalling how Kant understands the way we spontaneously and actively introduce rules into our construction of the experienced world, the reference in B to 'a necessary connection of perceptions' should not be too puzzling. The claim is in effect that our experience acquires its temporal dimension through the order we spontaneously impose on our intuitions in their relation to one another. Taken singly and independently of any relation to other things, no object has temporal dimension, so that must depend on the categories of relation, to wit, the categories of substance, causation and reciprocity. It is the first of these that works to secure the *duration* of what we experience, the second to secure *successiveness*, and the third to secure *simultaneity* or co-existence of objects of experience. It is the business of the immediately following three Analogies to make out the individual claims. We shall look at these three moves in turn and in slightly more detail than the mathematical principles attracted.

* * *

The First Analogy starts out from the thought that of necessity time persists. It does not stop and start. Its persistence is an essential feature of it. It determines the way in which we order intuition, for the persistence of time is only given to us objectively through the way in which we bring understanding to bear on the data of intuition. We might say that unless our intuitions are synthesized in the right way we wouldn't experience things in that temporal manner at all. But how is it that experience manifests that feature of time? We are supposing ourselves to start out from nothing more than the constantly changing flow of sensation, which is all that is materially given to us in intuition, and as bringing understanding to bear on that in the construction of objectively valid experience. The objective appearances that we arrive at either succeed one another or else they co-exist, and in either case they last for a certain time (enjoying necessary extensive temporal magnitude by the Axioms of Intuition). What is more, Kant thinks, the time in which our various appearances exist does not itself change, but is always one and the same, and that *a priori* truth has to be represented in our experience itself. Since time and its duration cannot be given to us directly – it is not itself material of our experience, but merely its form – we have to synthesize our intuition so that changes among appearances are seen as changing states of something underlying and unchanging, namely *substance*. As we do this, we introduce into our perceptual experience something that persists throughout all change and gives manifest experiential content to the durational aspect of time. In addition, Kant thinks the formality of time's persistence, its not stopping and starting, has to be secured experientially by our so organizing our intuitions that all their changes are viewed as changes in *one* underlying substance. A couple of remarks are in order here.

First, it is important that the persisting substance should be given to us in experience in one way or another. The formal concept *substance* has to have some empirical realization, and for Kant this is apparently *matter*, since in stating the Principle of Permanence of Substance (B225) he asserts, 'In all change of appearances substance is permanent; its quantum in nature is neither increased nor diminished', and what was thought to be conserved through all change was mass or matter.[6] However, even if the argument to a persisting substance were in order, the further step to the constancy of its quantum of matter or mass, or mass-energy as we have since come to think of it, is not secure. Why should the quantity of matter in a closed system not be a variable feature of it, so that at different times while the same world-whole persists, its material quantum oscillates around some fixed kernel?[7] Kant would have to say that under such a hypothesis we would lose the idea of a single persisting time; only as far as his argument goes, the idea of our synthesizing our intuitions in terms of a persisting substance of variable massiveness, matter of some quantity or other, would be enough to sustain that. The duration of time under such a regime does not seem directly under threat.

Secondly, as Kant is officially thinking, it would appear that our ordinary classificatory terms would need to be regarded as shorthand for ways of talking about qualities or accidents of persisting matter. Talk about the sun and the moon, or the objects closer to hand on my desk, would get reduced to talk about ways in which matter is qualified at different points in space and time. Now, there had indeed been philosophical precedent for this, notably in Spinoza's *Ethics*, where the objects of everyday speech are regarded as modes of the one necessarily existing substance and appearing to us either under the attribute of extension or that of thought. Only the precedent was not very promising. Spinoza's all-embracing substance does not easily lend itself to empirical introduction, and if we just concentrate on the attribute of extension, when we think through the task of identifying different points at which otherwise incompatible predicates can be instantiated (as in 'her hair is blond, whereas yours is auburn' or 'Jack goes downhill while Jill goes up'), we see that that demands the introduction of individuals located in places, and individuals that must themselves be thought of as persisting things, not as qualities or modes of some other substance, such as Cartesian extension.

In fairness to Kant, it can be said that in this Analogy he moves with some degree of insouciance between talk about *substance* and talk about *substances.* It does make better sense to hear him saying that for there to be change in the world there must be persisting *substances* (individual dogs, cats, and so on) whose states alter from moment to moment. Furthermore, it would be open to him to say the temporally extended existence of such things sufficiently overlapping one another in their span of existence is all we need if our experience is to be structured within a single time frame, and that is what is better thought of as being brought by the understanding to the *a priori* nature of the world.

What prevents Kant from adopting this more promising suggestion is that, quite apart from accounting for the temporality of appearances, the Analogies are meant to serve as the main strut in securing the status of the laws of classical physics and Newtonian mechanics as expressing material necessities, and not just contingent regularities that might break down. Central to classical physics are conservation laws, in particular, the conservation of mass, with its implication that matter can neither be created nor destroyed. Now, Kant certainly does not pretend to show that the fundamental laws hold as a matter of conceptual necessity, for that would make them analytic, and he is perfectly well aware that they are not that. What he does envisage doing is to show how we can think of them as empirically discovered ways in which the understanding handles the manifold of intuition in accordance with the requirement of objective validity. So, in the case in point, understanding has to order the world in terms of changing states of something permanent in order to introduce the persistence of time, and it needs to do so in terms of a single empirical substance if any conservation law can be said to acquire the necessity (= strict universality) that its being a law requires.

If I am right about this, we can understand Kant as being moved in two directions at once. A single persisting substance would indeed secure the objective persistence of time, though isn't the only way in which that can be achieved. Furthermore, the achievements of classical physics and mechanics seemed secure in Kant's day, and their claims to state strict laws looked to be in good order. So they must be empirical manifestations of the way in which the categories achieve objective validity or 'relation to an object'. What could be a more natural metaphysical suggestion, then, than to say that the category of substance is used to organize our experience in terms of the changing affections of some persisting empirical thing, to wit, matter, or in the guise of its constitutive attractive and repulsive forces? In that way, Kant not only has a good account of how our experience manifests the persistence of time, but also how the conservation laws of the exact sciences have the strict universality for us that they do. Given that dual target, one can appreciate the appeal to him of the proof he offers.

Before moving on to the Second Analogy it is interesting to reflect on the way Kant might have responded to Locke's notorious puzzlement a century earlier about substance, a treatment of the topic he never brings himself to mention. How is it, Locke wondered, that we use that concept in the explanation of what it is that has properties and unites them in individual objects, yet without any such thing being given to us in experience? The idea we form, he weakly suggested, is one which is unsatisfactorily 'obscure and relative' (*Essay*, II.xxiii.3). Kant's response to this would surely have been that Locke was looking in the wrong place, assuming that the idea of substance is a material idea, whereas in truth it is a purely formal one. Locke's conception of experience entailed that substance could not be located within the matter of sensation, but if only he had understood that we deploy that *a priori* concept in fashioning out of our manifold perceptions a world of persisting appearances, he would have had no cause for puzzlement. He would, of course, have had to admit that the concept *substance* is not empirically acquired, any more than the concepts *space* and *time*, but once his doctrinaire empiricism is left behind, he should have no qualms about the notion, and not think of us as condemned to irredeemable intellectual inadequacy at this sensitive point.

* * *

The Second Analogy confronts the general question how it is that the world we experience can possibly manifest the temporal directionality that is written into the form of inner sense. What makes it objectively the case that time advances, or that events succeed one another in a determinate order? The unacceptability of three answers to it makes the question particularly acute.

In the first place, as we have already seen in chapter 2, while our sensory apprehensions are given to us successively in time, that is not part of their empirical content. So the temporality of the world we experience, and which is largely constructed out of that content, cannot be something that is directly given to us in perception. 'Time cannot be outwardly intuited, any more than space can be intuited as something in us' (A23/B37). Nor can objective temporal succession be understood as a direct reflection of the order of our apprehending things, since so often we have no choice but to view objectively simultaneous states of affairs one after the other.

Still less is it open to us to say that the temporal succession of appearances is the temporality of the world as it is in itself. It has already been established that that world lies beyond our ken, and so could neither be what our experience of temporal flow is of, nor could its putative 'temporality' explain the successive character of the objective states of affairs and events that appear to us. Anyway, as we have seen, Kant is quite definite that, applied to things in themselves, temporal, spatial and other such terms 'would carry with them quite other meanings, and would not apply to appearances as possible objects of experience' (A206/B252).

His way of avoiding these snares starts off from a consideration of how we distinguish between subjectively apprehending things in a certain order and objectively apprehending a certain order in things. Understanding how this distinction comes to be made then allows him to say how it is that the world of nature conforms to that aspect of the temporal form of intuition that is its constant successiveness, its continuous advance from one moment to the next. In a nutshell, the crucial thought is that temporal order is the order that is imported into experience by the category of causation, so that successively ordered apprehensions are only apprehensions of two successively ordered events or states of affairs if what is apprehended is synthesized by the understanding in the light of some causal rule under which those events are taken to fall. To bring the manifold of appearances under a causal law both imposes a necessary order on the appearances so synthesized and also explains the phenomenon by which, within the continuously successive flow of our intuitions, we distinguish between perceptions of simultaneity and perceptions of succession.

By extension, the natural world is through and through successive in virtue of being subject to universal causal determinism. As the Principle of the Second Analogy states it, 'All alteration takes place in conformity with the law of the connection of cause and effect' (B232), where 'alteration' picks out alteration or change in the world rather than in our changing apprehensions of it. At the end of this discussion, we shall see how this Analogy, like the previous one and the two mathematical Principles, makes its own contribution to the philosophical grounding of natural science.

While the flow of sensation is itself always successive, very often we are disinclined to think that we have to do with a succession of events or states of affairs. When I perceive two faces of a house, front and rear, as I walk round it, I recognize that I have seen, one after the other, different co-existing sides of the same building. It would have made no difference to what I experienced had I on that occasion walked around the property in the other direction, viewing first the rear, and only then the front. In other cases, though, things are not like that. I see you strike the match and then I see the gas light, and take myself thereby to see successive events, not simultaneous ones. In such a case, Kant takes it that our perceptions could not have occurred in the reverse order, and it is that that testifies to the objective order of the events perceived.

To understand what is going on, it is as well to go slowly. First, let us not misunderstand the irreversibility which is of such importance for Kant. We are concerned with apprehensions of token events, not of event types. It is not that in the first sort of case while the particular event concerned was a viewing of the house that took place in the order F–G, there could perfectly well be other house viewings occurring in the reverse order, G–F, whereas in the observations of the gas lighting that is not so. That could not be what Kant had in mind, since obviously enough matches can be observed being struck after the gas is seen to be lit. (The housewife mistakenly thinks her first attempt to light the stove has failed, and so she strikes a second match.) And even if that sort of example were forestalled and given sufficient specificity so there were only apprehensions of type F followed by ones of type G, that by itself would not suggest for a moment why on a particular occasion of such a uniform series there should be any necessary succession among particular token apprehensions. (It would certainly not do to say that it is definitional of that apprehending of the striking match being the one it was that it should have preceded the particular perception of the gas catching light that makes the ordering an irreversible one. That move would have the effect of making all subjectively successive apprehensions necessary, even those of the two sides of the house. Anyway the supposed necessity there is of quite the wrong kind.)

What Kant must have meant is that the particular objective states of affairs or events we are concerned with, and which are assumed to be identified independently of any reference to our observing them, could, on the occasion of my viewing them in the order F–G, in some cases just as well have been observed in the reverse order; by contrast, in other cases the order of apprehension could only have been reversed on that occasion if states of affairs had been differently arranged. For me first to have seen the gas light, then seen the match struck, would only have been possible if the objective situation had been other than in fact it was. Since we are concerned with the order of apprehensions on this occasion and not some other one, that must be the irreversibility or necessary succession with which we have to deal.

Secondly, we should misunderstand Kant if we were to take the phenomenon of irreversibility of perceptions as itself somehow constituting the successive nature of the events perceived. Rather, it is a test we can use to tell or discern when we are perceiving objective succession, a criterion in the old sense of a means of telling. A193/B238 expresses the idea by saying 'we must derive the *subjective succession* of apprehension from the *objective succession* of appearances', where the derived 'subjective succession' is not so much its successiveness, which is given directly in intuition, as the necessity, or irreversibility, of the order of those apprehensions. Obviously enough, if the irreversibility were being relied on in some way to account for the objective order of the events perceived, it would be blatantly circular to derive it from the objective succession of those very events. On the other hand, if the objective succession naturally gives rise to irreversibility, then awareness of irreversibility will be an excellent index of real succession. We 'derive' the subjective irreversibility from the objective succession in that the former is fully explained by the latter.

That does of course leave the question open how it is that the objective flow of events gets constituted in our synthesizing of the manifold. The answer is supplied for Kant by whatever it is that the understanding makes use of to generate the irreversibility of apprehensions. As he sees it, that can only be the category of causality, which subjects the manifold of appearance to a necessary rule, viz. a rule according to which upon the occurrence of one event another necessarily and invariably follows. Hence we are told: 'The objective succession will therefore consist in that order of the manifold of appearance [= the objective world, A.S.] according to which, *in conformity with a rule*, the apprehension of that which happens follows upon the apprehension of that which precedes. Thus only can I be justified in asserting, not merely of my apprehension, but of appearance itself, that a succession is to be met with in it' (A193/B238).

At first one might suspect that Kant is smuggling succession far too easily into the necessity that the notion of causation brings with it. After all, he himself is willing to acknowledge that 'the great majority of efficient natural causes are simultaneous with their effects' (A203/B248). And does not the Third Analogy account for objective simultaneity in terms of reciprocal instantaneous causality? These two reflections can makes it look very much as if causality and succession are at best contingently and loosely related and not necessarily and strictly so, which is what Kant is relying on at this point of the argument.

We shall return to these points shortly, but what is important at the moment is to remember that the notion of causality that is in play here is the *schematized* category, the category as brought to bear on intuitions that are given to us in the form of inner sense that is Time. And since it is an unavoidable and hence necessary feature of the flow of intuition that it is successive, that feature of it is bound to be preserved in the synthesis of it by which the understanding comes to construct the world of appearances. This is just one more specific application of the Highest Principle of synthetic judgement that has it that 'the conditions of the *possibility of experience* in general [viz. the successive nature of all sensory stimuli, A.S.] are likewise conditions of the *possibility of objects of experience* [viz. successiveness among events and states of affairs]' (A158/B197). As we synthesize the given manifold of intuition in terms of hypothetical judgements by means of the category of causation we bring them under a necessary rule to the effect that the occurrence of the term that answers to the antecedent of the judgement must be accompanied by an occurrence of a term fitting the consequent. And while there is no allusion to successiveness in that way of putting it, it is brought into the picture as soon as we realize that what is brought under a rule are intuitions that are themselves ineluctably successive. That is what makes the necessarily *accompanying* occurrence that fits the consequent a necessarily *successive* occurrence.

The two issues I rather brusquely brushed aside can now be addressed. As for the reciprocal causality of the Third Analogy, the right thing to say is that there we are dealing with the schematized form of a different category than here, the category of community (reciprocity between agent and patient), not that of causality and dependence. Lest this observation be thought to be just empty verbiage and to ignore the centrality of causation in Kant's idea of community, his thought in the Second Analogy can be taken to be focused exclusively on unidirectional causality, for it is only that and not bi-directional causality that gives rise to the phenomenon of irreversibility in our perceptions, and so it is only that which is implicated in our understanding of objective succession.

The other point is more serious. Kant has no hesitation is admitting that much unidirectional causality is simultaneous, not successive, and he is obviously vexed. What he says is that even though we experience no lapse of time between, say, laying a leaden ball on a stuffed cushion and the appearance of a hollow in the material, none the less the causality of the rule orders the events in time. 'I still distinguish the two [cause and effect, A.S.] through the time-relation of their dynamical connection' (A203/B248). What is difficult to understand though is how there may be succession without lapse of time ('a vanishing quantity', ibid.). I suggest that what Kant may have had in mind is something like the following. Assertions about the simultaneity of cause and effect are made on the basis of everyday experience and usually without the aid of more sensitive instrumentation like stop-watches or atomic clocks.

Naturally, very often we say things are simultaneous when a more refined judgement would not concur. In the case of the ball and the cushion and its like, the causal laws at work involve mechanical forces, and the exertion of force and the transmission of energy are always temporally directed. Strictly speaking then, there is no true unidirectional causality where cause and effect are simultaneous. Our saying that there is is merely a reflection of our lack of acuity in the temporal judgements we are prone to make. So really there is no succession without lapse of time, but very often there is succession without our being able to discern lapse of time. Taken in that way, the ball and the cushion example poses no serious threat to Kant's ingenious proposal. And as he says, 'if I lay the ball on the cushion, a hollow follows upon the previously flat smooth shape; but if (for any reason) there previously exists a hollow in the cushion, a leaden ball does not follow upon it' (A203/B249).

There are, of course, other questions to ask. A critic might object that even if the irreversibility is our guide to temporal succession, what Kant says is that it results from our having brought intuitions under a strict rule. Now maybe we have indeed done something of the kind in the gas lighting case, but it is stretching things too far to suggest that the same is true in that of the ship making its passage downstream or the leaden ball on its velvet cushion. There is no reason to suppose that our ability to order the relevant events in time supposes we have any grasp of causal laws that might explain the fixed order of our apprehensions. How then can we seriously suppose that the category of causality is really doing the work Kant assigns to it?

The complaint is correct enough in its way, but it should not worry Kant or his more generous-minded readers overmuch. While the dynamical Principles of Understanding, the Analogies and the Postulates, are constitutive of the objective realm, they are merely regulative of our perception of it. So we may look to synthesize our experience by reference to or in conformity with strict laws without being able to formulate them with any degree of precision. Finding our perceptions to be irreversible is something we do whether or not we know in the particular case just what makes them so, and can be seen as a justification for our optimism that we shall eventually be able to find and formulate laws under which the ordered events we perceive can be brought. To order those events in time does not suppose that we are already in possession of such laws, merely that we exercise understanding in their conceptualization in such a way that they can be or can come to be related under appropriate causal laws in our ulterior investigation of the world.

The same reflection can be usefully brought to bear on what might seem another objection to Kant's procedure, namely that we plainly order events as successive which are causally unconnected with one another. The housewife lit the gas before the ship left harbour. Let us protreptically grant Kant the idea of objective simultaneity that he comes to put in place in the Third Analogy. Then the thought would be that pairs of causally unrelated successive events are so ordered because one or both members of the pairs are simultaneous with other events which are causally related to the pairs' members. So the lighting of the gas brought the water to boil, and the ship left harbour just then. The lighting of the gas preceded the water's boiling, and so, by the Kantian route, was followed by the causally unrelated weighing of anchor. Again the irreversibility of the perception of the gas's lighting and the ship's leaving harbour is testimony to our being confident of finding some such linking causal laws as over time we build up a firmer understanding of the workings of the world we experience.

The prime aim of this Analogy is to establish that all alterations (changes in the state of things) are governed by causal law. That should follow from a proof that all events (changes in things' states) are preceded by others. Then, by this account of temporal succession, each one must be the effect of some earlier one under one causal law or another. What must consequently be ruled out then is that there should be some first event in the flow of appearances, though this requirement need not stretch to the world as it is in itself, which Kant envisages as being possibly brought into existence by what must be an act of God's intellectual intuition (A206/B251–2 together with B138–9). Secondly, there must be no anomalous events, anomalous in the sense of events that can be dated by their simultaneity with others that do, under some intrinsic description of them, fall under causal laws, yet which themselves do not.

As for the first matter, Kant tells us that that something happens cannot be perceived unless it is preceded by an appearance which does not contain that state. For 'an event which should follow upon an empty time . . . is as little capable of being apprehended as empty time itself' (A192/B237). I suppose that the idea is that it is already ruled out as impossible that empty time should be intuited. In that case, we could not intuit some appearance after having done the impossible. What though if someone says: a child has its first intuitions, but not after intuiting nothing, only after there being no earlier intuition, so why shouldn't there be a first uncaused event, or one which is preceded by no other – say the Big Bang? Kant certainly says that there can be beginning of series (like the series of the infant's intuitions), but no beginning of the empirical world itself. Perhaps he would say that it is regulative of our understanding that we seek for a cause of anything, and that this will involve us in supposing that for any event there will be a preceding one. Only under that condition will our experience of the world enjoy full objective validity. I shall not pursue the issue.

The second point is not discussed in the Analogy, possibly because it didn't occur to Kant as needing to be circumvented. His usual line when confronted with problems of this order is to say that events that do not fit into the causal flow are ruled out by their failing to comply with the supreme principle, the transcendental unity of apperception. And at A206 we do find him saying: 'any first uncaused event...cannot be admitted as an event among appearances, since its mere possibility would destroy the unity of experience' (A206/B251). I could not be aware of such things as entering into the general flow of the life I recognize as mine. But that move is not available to cope with the sorts of anomaly under consideration now, since we have already made room for them within my self-conscious life by supposing them to be experientially simultaneous with things that do enter into the causal flow. That route then is blocked. Another one is open though. Such events are, it is supposed, ones I could apprehend: then, just because there is a distinction between the objects of my knowledge and my knowledge of them (A104, A191/B236), there will need to be a causal link between those objects and my perceptual system just as there is between the causally integrated events they are simultaneous with and other events that can appear to me. The very idea of their being given to me in intuition itself ensures that they are not anomalous under all descriptions under which they are rightly brought.

One can even imagine Kant drawing on what he over-optimistically takes himself to have established in the First Analogy to strengthen the argument of the Second at this point. While he has no claim to have shown that any world we might experience is a material world, he does think it must be substantial. (The material being defined, I take it, by the empirical laws governing whatever substance we are given to experience, for Kant those of classical mechanics.) The Principles argue that any world-substance must obey laws that hold universally within that world. In that case our would-be anomalous events, being particular modal manifestations of the one persisting substance Kant presumes there to be, will necessary fall under whatever basic laws govern it in its empirical realization. Even if we don't know what those laws are, we have every reason to suppose as a matter of transcendental necessity that they apply unrestrictedly. Ergo, no anomalies.

The First Analogy laid the metaphysical foundation for natural science by showing it internal to objective experience that it be governed by some fundamental necessity of conservation. Failing that, experience could not exhibit the persistence of time that our sensibility requires. Now the Second Analogy performs a similar task for Newton's first law, the law of inertia. Objects' momentum is constant unless they are acted on by outside forces. All changes in direction or velocity have to be accounted for in terms of external causes, where the regularities involved are strict and exceptionless, and not merely extensively applicable. As before, it is no part of Kant's intention to derive the empirical law as a metaphysical truth. What he does see philosophy as having to do is to show how the laws that are empirically discovered can be accounted such. Their strict universality is inherited from the abstract claim that in making the successive nature of time manifest throughout experience we are obliged to synthesize our apprehensions through the categories in a way that makes all events and all alterations of state subject to deterministic laws. This is Kant's homage to the principle of sufficient reason (A201/B246). That is a synthetic *a priori* truth, one of the proper discoveries of pure reason, but the particular ways in which that principle comes to be realized for creatures with our mental endowments is an empirical matter that belongs to the realm of natural, not speculative, philosophy. As he put it towards the end of the Transcendental Deduction:

> Pure understanding is not in a position, through mere categories, to pre-scribe to appearances any *a priori laws* other than those which are involved in a *nature in general*, that is, in the conformity to law of all appearances in space and time. Special laws, as concerning those appearances which are empirically determined, cannot in their specific character be *derived from* the categories, although they are one and all subject to them. To obtain any knowledge whatever of these special laws, we must resort to experience, but it is the *a priori* laws alone that can instruct us in regard to experience in general, and as to what it is that can be known as an object of experience. (B165)

It is fundamentally for this reason that Kant is content to claim that 'however exaggerated and absurd it may sound, it is nonetheless quite correct to say that understanding is the source of Nature's laws' (A127).

Just as with the First Analogy Kant had a response to Locke's puzzle-ment about substance, so with the Second he has what he takes to be needed to solve Hume's problem about causation: how it is that the necessities of causal order get into the natural world. What the world shows up independently of the way in which we handle it are only regularities, there are no necessities. Yet without necessity there is no causality, and without causality, no objective time ordering, and without that, no unity of apperception. So, where there is necessity, and has to be so, we must look to ourselves to provide it. In this way, our spontaneous ordering of things in ways that are strictly universal and *a priori* (that is, imported by ourselves) amounts to the necessity that so bemused Hume. As was the case with Locke on the topic of substance, Kant will respond to Hume by saying that the necessity he was looking for eluded him just because the only place he thought it might be found was guaranteed to exclude it, and where it was he did not think to look.

At this point Hume's ghost can well be imagined dubiously enquiring of Kant just how it is that he supposes any ordering we engage in could possibly secure more than regular concomitances that cannot be protected against future breakdown. It is a question to which Kant must imperatively supply an answer. The necessity of a rule is nothing other than its strict, exceptionless universality. And that can only be distinguished in our experience from constant regularity if we recognize it to be the outcome of the spontaneous employment of our understanding. It may well be that unless there were regularities in the order of repeated intuitions we should be unable to synthesize objects in a rule-governed way (and hence, by the Transcendental Deduction, cease to enjoy genuine experience at all), but the mere occurrence of regularity can never provide more than 'comparative universality, that is, extensive applicability' (A91–2, 112–13, 196/B124, 241). Strict universality comes only with our determination to treat a regularity as a necessity; it results from our 'subjecting the representations to a rule, and in so necessitating us to connect them in some specific manner' (A197/B242). That, it appears, is something that depends on us, although it is something we have to do in one way or another if we are to have objective experience at all. Thus: 'Only in so far as our representations are necessitated in a certain order as regards their time-relations do they acquire objective meaning' (ibid.).

In what way, then, Hume's ghost might go on to ask, could it be up to us spontaneously to 'subject our representation to a necessary rule'? Kant is never explicit enough about this, and there seems to be only one answer available to him. It is that we identify some regularities in our apprehensions as providing a constructive base in our ordering of the manifold, one that enables us to make reasonable sense of new incoming experience as long as it holds, and then, as it comes to occupy more and more of a weight-bearing role in the picture of the world we progressively build up, so we become less and less willing to relinquish it and to allow it to break down. We make adjustments elsewhere in the developing system of our understanding so that the regularity is not disturbed, and at the limit our preference takes the form of a determination to treat the regularity as one that nothing will shake. At that point mere comparative universality has given way to necessity and strict universality, regularity to necessary rule, association to affinity. Only thus can Hume's ghost be laid to rest.

* * *

The Third, and last, Analogy introduces the idea of objective co-existence among appearances, and confronts the same sort of problem as the Second: How can we introduce a notion of simultaneity when the things we think of as co-existing are so often only perceived in succession? The farther target that Kant has in view is a metaphysical underpinning for Newton's law of universal gravitation, according to which every particle attracts every other with a force proportional to the product of their masses and inversely proportional to the square of the distance between their centres. For that to hold, every particular evidently has to be in reciprocal community with every other, and it is that general transcendental necessity which Kant seeks to establish here.

The proof structure employs much the same considerations as before. If objective time ordering requires that there be causal links between earlier and later events, then objective simultaneity requires that there be necessary, strictly universal, two-way causal links. As the understanding is obliged to synthesize data in line with the requirements of the structure of time, we are bound to institute bi-directional unbreakable regularities in our experience. As before, of course, we do not draw upon them explicitly whenever we are inclined to judge things as co-existing or talk of events as taking place simultaneously, but in the absence of things and events conforming to some law of reciprocal causality, the temporal claims we make would not hold, or, perhaps better, could not be introduced and sustained. Either we would mistakenly have judged simultaneous two events that were successive, or we should have failed to make sense of the manifold of intuition in a way that attained to any respectable degree of objectivity. Our attempt to employ understanding in making objective sense of the way the world impinges upon our senses would have run into a dead end in either case.

* * *

Kant summarizes what he has achieved in the Analogies by saying that they 'declare that all appearances lie, and must lie, in *one nature*, because without this *a priori* unity no unity of experience, and therefore no determination of objects in it, would be possible' (A216/B263). It should by now be clear enough how this has been made out. Understanding has to order the manifold of sense in such a way as to conform with the *a priori* structure of time and space. That structure must be made manifest through what is given to us in experience, so, in the case of time-order, the things and events we construct as objects of perception must conform to the various necessities just outlined. So too must those things we do not, or cannot, perceive directly, but whose interactions with one another have actual or potential perceptual consequences for us (cf. A231).

Does this mean then that the empirical laws that the exact sciences discover are themselves *a priori*? Strange though it may seem, since strict universality is a criterion (here, surely, sufficient condition) of the *a priori* (B3–4), the answer must be 'Yes', but only in the modest sense that it is up to us to uphold them by refusing to count anything as an exception or a decisive counter-example to a proposed law.[8] As we have seen Kant making plain, that does not mean that they can be dreamed up in the study without investigating the world (of appearance) itself – in that sense they are *a posteriori*; nor does it imply that they enjoy any sort of conceptual necessity. That cannot be so if for no other reason than that it is an evident logical possibility that the particular laws which we discover (or invent) might not have held, whereas others, quite unknown to us, might have done so, and in full conformity with the Analogies.[9]

In the last of the Pure Principles, the Postulates of Empirical Thought, Kant insists that the requirements of understanding cannot be guaranteed any realization. And we have already seen him mentioning a situation in which they wouldn't be realized, namely, in a chaotic world, which couldn't be a world for us. When we do find a realization of the Principles, that does not formally exclude there being others. Whether there are or not is not something for understanding to determine independently of intuition (A230/B282–3). All we can say is that any actuality that experience might reveal must conform to the Principles of Understanding. When we find regularities that appear to do so systematically, we have something approximating to objectivity in our overall picture of the world, where full objectivity is thought of not as truth itself, but as the best estimate of it that it is possible for us to come to.

We can, of course, imagine that had our perceptions been quite different, the familiar empirical laws we know might not have held. However, relative to the manifolds we actually have, and can actually have, Kant seems to think that they could only be successfully synthesized in the ways that Newtonian science prescribes, and that any alternatives we might come up with would be clearly inferior. Over time we have collectively struggled to secure systematic coherence for our understanding of the world, and with Newtonian science Kant takes it that we have at last succeeded. Asking the question about other real possibilities for doing that would be asking about perceptions that are not our own, and for Kant this is not something we are in a position to say anything about, partly because the material concepts we would need to possess to articulate such possibilities are not supplied by the manifold with which we are in fact presented (cf. A206, B251–2). Speculation about such matters is idle, though once we allow for that possibility we may have to acknowledge that 'the objective validity of our judgments is limited' (A286/B342–3).

This concession of Kant's should not be misunderstood. As it occurs here it is not the thought that if the world is given to other, non-human, sensibilities in ways it is not given to ours, that impugns the objectivity of our judgements. They are made about the way in which we should best understand the world as it presents itself to us, and how it strikes others hardly bears on that. What would be in question is whether we are justified in supposing that the world of appearance lies open in its totality to us in our best systematic way of understanding it. The answer must be that we have no very good reason to think that it does. Our grasp of the world of appearance may only be a grasp of part of the appearing world; but the grasp of that part is not rendered a partial grasp just because it is not the grasp of the whole. So the limitation of the objective validity of our judgements appears to be no more than its being limited to the way in which the world is given to appear to us. However, as we shall shortly see, this may not be the last thing to say on this score.

The Principles, then, tell us at an extremely high level of generality what any world of appearances we could enjoy must be like. It must lend itself to measurement; it must be extensively and intensively continuous (no vacua, no ultimate atoms), and in consequence of its inevitable spatio-temporality, its fundamental constituents will be governed by a conservation law and conform to the demands of inertia and ubiquitous causal community (in our case, the equality of action and reaction and universal gravitation). Claims like these lie far away from the self-conscious experience of most of us as we go about our daily business, and given that they ultimately derive from the application of the categories to what sensibility provides, it is entirely in order to ask what relation Kant must have supposed there to be between these large global claims and the more homely experiential beliefs we have that lay claim to objective validity and truth.

Clearly the construction of a way of understanding the world that conforms to the Principles is not a matter for the individual, and the importance of Newton in Kant's field of vision is likewise testimony to its not being the work of a single generation. So, the best suggestion must be that we have to see our claims to objective validity for our everyday beliefs as conditionally subject to the demand that they permit of integration within a system of natural science that conforms to the Principles and comes to be elaborated over time. When I observe that the dogs are asleep or that the trains are running punctually, these thoughts can only be fully justified if my experiential judgements can be found a place in an understanding of the world that runs along the lines that the Principles specify and which commands the assent of others who are 'possessed of reason' (A820/B848). However, the individual subject's deep ignorance of the workings of classical mechanics won't be a bar to his everyday beliefs, not cast in such terms, being both objectively valid and straightforwardly true.

As Kant represents them, the Principles specify no empirical laws, but are only formal requirements that whatever empirical laws we do discover must satisfy if they can be made into rules that generate objectivity. Nevertheless, this mild way of presenting them does not deprive them of purchase over our close-to-home picture of the world, for as we make sense of our immediate surroundings, and, indeed, even of ourselves, should it turn out that our homely beliefs resist incorporation within a systematic and scientific account of our surroundings, we would be under pressure to revise them, and so to treat as false what initially seemed so evident. That possibility, though, must be a fairly remote one, since the construction of a systematic way of understanding nature has to start out from making sense of our everyday, close-to-home beliefs. To overturn those in any large measure would risk depriving ourselves of the very thing we need to get the larger system off the ground. (This is of course emphatically not to imply that we should still believe the earth is flat.)

Then, too, the Principles state no more than singly necessary conditions on objective validity, not sufficient ones, even when taken jointly. That is, it seems an open possibility that there should be various competing ways in which they might be satisfied, and if they were themselves supposed to be definitive of objective validity, there would be a risk of incoherence. Empirical data might support either of two or more constructions, each one conforming to the Principles, yet each at odds with the others. Such would have been the situation that presented itself as Ptolemaic cosmology confronted its Copernican rival, or when, at a much later date, classical physics confronted relativity theory, and classical mechanics, quantum mechanics, as long as in each case we find ourselves restricting attention to the range of phenomena that the earlier established system had taken for its support.

Kant is aware of the need to say more here, and he develops his position considerably later in the *Critique*, in an Appendix to the Transcendental Dialectic that he entitles 'The Regulative Employment of the Ideas of Pure Reason' (A642–68/B670–96). Just as the Principles were concerned with the way in which Understanding is constrained in its handling the matter of sensibility, here we see how the transcendental demands of a third faculty of the mind, Reason, direct Understanding in its successful operation. Kant's idea is simple enough: it is a demand of reason that the constructions of the understanding be maximally systematic, and the ideal of systematicity expresses itself in our fashioning the world of appearances as a system of Nature whose unity is characterized by a parsimony of principles that enjoy maximal extension.[10] So, as we are confronted with the question of choice between global scientific theories of the world of appearance that compete over the same range of data and which all satisfy the Pure Principles of Understanding, that theory which enjoys greatest systematic unity (fewest basic principles, greatest extensive range) is that which has strongest claim to objectivity. As Kant puts it: 'the systematic unity of the knowledge [supplied by, A.S.] understanding is *the criterion of the truth* of its rules' (A647/B675). Adding this condition to the previous necessary ones seemingly gives him what he takes to be a sufficient evidential test of the correctness of the wider picture of the world that has been built up over time.[11]

Here we have more than just a methodological recommendation. That is, Kant takes it to be a transcendental requirement on the objective construction of appearances that this systematizing demand of reason be satisfied. He writes: 'The law of reason which requires us to seek for this unity, is a necessary law, since without it we should have no reason at all, and without reason no coherent employment of the understanding, and in the absence of this, no sufficient criterion of empirical truth. In order therefore, to secure an empirical criterion we have no option save to presuppose the systematic unity of nature as objectively valid and necessary' (A651/B679).[12]

This is as clear a statement as we are given of the view that the necessity of the Principles supplemented by the necessity of the rule of reason gives us a sufficient evidential condition of the truth of a total world picture. But we need to be careful. At any moment we might have to choose between two competing theories, rejecting one as false on account of its apparently imperfect systematicity. However, that cannot guarantee that the rival, more comprehensive, view of the world is itself correct, since we have no assurance that the future will not throw up yet new data that call for a revised, even more inclusive, theory which will oust the previous temporary victor. Indeed, Kant suggests that finding an ideally unified theory is nothing other than a constant challenge since it always directs our attention to novel observations, to 'cases which are not given', in the search for still greater coherence (A647/B675).

At this point we are told that the employment of the idea of systematicity is regulative rather than constitutive of experience.[13] It isn't constitutive, since it has no determinate content, yet, as Kant says, 'it has an excellent and indeed indispensably necessary regulative employment, namely that of directing the understanding towards a certain goal upon which the routes marked out by all its rules converge, as upon their point of intersection. This point is indeed a mere Idea, a *focus imaginarius*, from which, since it lies quite outside the bounds of possible experience, the concepts of the understanding do not proceed; nonetheless it serves to give to these concepts the greatest possible unity combined with the greatest possible extension' (A644/B673).

These two passages need to be consistent. It can easily look as if Kant is saying both that if there is to be an empirical criterion (= test) of truth, it will be the most systematic possible construction of experience, but also that the idea of such a system is not real, but merely ideal; it is one which we can only approach asymptotically, ever more closely, but without ever reaching (A663/B691). Then the thought would be that we have better reason to suppose that the more systematic construction of the world is a closer approximation to the truth, but of no particular construction that we arrive at could we reasonably think that it will on that account be true, since we would always have to suppose that yet greater systems will remain to be achieved. The danger is that, seen from this high vantage point, our best tests for truth at any particular time look bound to be systematically out of line with what they are introduced as tests for.

Happily, there is a way of avoiding too great distress at this point. Kant seems to be saying, on the one hand, that if the idea of objective validity is to have real purchase, as it must if cognitive experience is to be possible, there must be a maximal systematization of the world that will handle all data that are really (materially) possible for us.[14] This comes to the thought that there must be a moment at which physics is a completed science, for then the understanding will have elaborated a view of the world that accommodates all cases that our receptivity to the world in itself is liable to throw up. All that will happen thereafter will be that we come upon hitherto unconsidered cases of things that actually fit within the framework of that completed scientific edifice without challenging it.

Nevertheless, and on the other hand, while the notion of maximal systematicity is constitutive for fully objective experience, it is regulative for our conduct of investigating the world. We should always seek out greater systematicity and be alert to novel cases, 'cases which are not given', with an eye to rendering the whole more coherent (A647/B675). It may even be that when we have arrived at the point at which maximal coherence has actually been found, it will still be a logical possibility that even greater coherence should be found, and as far as logic is concerned the idea of maximal systematicity is indeed a *focus imaginarius* 'lying quite outside the bounds of possible experience'.[15] Yet that does nothing to contradict the thought that the point of *actual* maximum coherence can lie *within* the bounds of experience (and that can be allowed without our saying that its lying within the bounds of experience is itself a matter of experience). If this way of avoiding the apparent conflict is viable, as I take it to be, it will merely be an analogue of Kant's own claim that the dynamical Principles are regulative for intuition but constitutive of experience itself (A180, 664/B223, 692).

To implement this idea we need to keep apart the idea of fully objective validity itself and that of reasonable belief. Kant may well take it that the idea of objective validity requires there to be a unique, maximally coherent and systematic scientific account of the world into which all true everyday beliefs fit. At the same time, he may think that at almost any stage of the community's non-individualistic construction of the world, we shall have reason to believe that progress still remains to be made. The upshot will be that while in Kant's own day Newtonian science was extraordinarily impressive, the door is left open to rejection of it in the light of future discoveries which could not then be foreseen and which none the less left the phenomenal world fully temporal, as did in fact happen. As already noted, this need not threaten the objective validity of much of Kant's own everyday thought, since that will be (and we must expect it to be) smoothly incorporated within future theoretical advance, such advance having itself to be built on truths about observation and reliable beliefs about the surroundings in which observation takes place.

Another idea that I have said should be distinguished from that of objective validity is that of truth. Kant is consistent throughout the *Critique* in endorsing a correspondence conception of truth (A58/B82, A191/B236, A821/B849), and for all the importance of his insistence on coherence and system, that is always a norm of judgement and never definitive of truth itself. Just as is the case with the common agreement that we find among people's judgements, so too it is with our judgements' systematicity. Both serve as evidential tests of truth because they can be presumed to 'rest upon the common ground, namely, upon the object' (A821/B849). But just as people may agree on falsehood, so too high degrees of cohesion and system, viz. objective validity, may lie at a large distance from truth itself, and may not agree with or be grounded on 'the object'.

How, though, can Kant possibly maintain that distinction? In the Transcendental Deduction 'the object' was nothing other than intuition synthesized under the guidance of the categories. And the developing discussion has led to the thought that fully objective validity consists in the construction of 'the object' in the light of the Principles and the transcendental demand of Reason. In that case, appeal to 'the object' is already made in explicating the idea of objective validity, so it cannot serve a second time to distinguish truth from that. What this teaches must be that, as it appears here, 'the object' should be taken in another way entirely, namely as referring to what it is that appearances are ultimately appearances of, to wit, the world-in-itself that supplies us with the manifold of sensibility and which we come to represent through the forms of intuition and understanding as objective appearances.[16] Object-ively valid judgement then is, for Kant, true judgement when and only when it rests upon this common ground, and, as he says, 'it is for this reason that they [the judgements of different subjects, A.S.] are all in agreement with the object – the truth of the judgment being thereby proved' (ibid.).

In the course of constructing a systematic representation of the world we often accommodate some recalcitrance to our going best theory by emending the system. Rather than finding ways of preventing familiar generalizations from being defeated, we accept their defeat when we have a better proposal to hand or when we cannot in all consistency hold on to them and are forced to look for something better. There can also be situations in which choice between theories is less assured. An established theory may face some recalcitrance that an alternative theory does not; only the novel theory has the disadvantage that it fails to accommodate something that poses no problem for its rival. In that situation, the best Kantian response would be that neither theory is optimal, and that there is *prima facie* reason to suppose that a better alternative than either remains to be found, particularly if we are persuaded that the discordant observations cannot be brushed under the carpet and still demand their place within an acceptable overall picture of the world.

Let us now suppose that we advance to a point where we have a systematic theory that seems coherent and is to all intents and purposes an all-embracing GUT (grand universal theory) or TOE (theory of every-thing), hitherto, of course, a mere chimera. At such a point, we might think that physics has come to an end, particularly if, when we turn to what Kant calls 'cases that are not given', all we find are new instances of things we have already encountered, not instances of the strange un-known, or if quite new, then all easily accommodable within the going GUT or TOE. At this point there will be a strong temptation to say that we have a representation of the world of appearance that is maximally coherent and systematic and which can lay claim to absolute objectivity and truth. However, before we can accept that thought on Kant's behalf two countervailing considerations must be blocked.

First, someone might say that there is nothing to stop one supposing that alternative systematizations of the world might be built up that are equally coherent and extensive. Wouldn't it be the case that we would then have competing candidates for the optimal representation of the world? However, what the objector has to make out is that the rivals are more than notational variants of one another (as say expressions of one theory in different languages, or theories adopting different scales of measurement such as Fahrenheit/Celsius or Imperial/Metric). If they are genuine rivals, the Kantian should say that we are just back in the position of the last paragraph but one, and that, *contra* the hypothesis, the envisaged theories are both sub-optimal. On the other hand, if they are not actual or potential rivals, they must be notational variants of one another, and so pose no threat.

Secondly, we should return the issue of alternative views of the world, alternatives not now for us, as we were contemplating in the last paragraphs, but for other possible beings whose mode of receptive intuition (quasi-sensibility) is distinctly unlike our own. This is not to take up the question that, with Kant, I dismissed as idle before, namely whether there are such others, and if so how appearances might be for them. It is rather whether the possibility of their existence poses any deep threat to our own experience attaining to full objectivity and truth. As we saw above, what Kant actually says is that if there are such beings, then they may have things as their objects and the objective validity of our own judgements is in consequence liable to be limited. We need to know whether that apparent concession (A286/B342–3) can be treated in quite the benign way I previously suggested Kant would have us believe.[17]

Life would be at its simplest if any such possibility could just be dismissed as illusory. First of all, we know that by 'other forms of sensibility' is not meant spatio-temporal sensibility different from ours just in giving rise to secondary quality experience of sorts quite alien to us, experience of the kind that bees and bats are known to have. That cannot be what is in question, because Kant is firm about rejecting what he calls 'mere modifications of our senses' as genuine properties of objects (appearances) (A29/B45).[18] So what is under consideration has to be intuition that is other than spatio-temporal yet passive and receptive none the less, not purely active, spontaneous and intellectual.[19] Furthermore, we are supposing such experience to arise out of contact with the same range of things-in-themselves as we ourselves are receptively exposed to, so we ought to be focusing on other subjects who enjoy intuitive experience and in doing so enjoy a range of appearances that we do not. Even so, we must suppose that the appearances they have access to are 'outer' to them (that is, of something distinct from themselves) (A23/B38). Putting these various things together, that requires that these others' experience enables them to identify and re-identify such appearances as come their way, and that would seem to be impossible in the absence at least of time, and also, if not of space itself, of something closely analogous to it.[20] In that case, the conclusion within reach would be that no such beings as are envisaged could exist, and hence that no threat from that quarter is posed to the potential completeness of our view of the world of appearance's objects.

That, however, is not the line that Kant takes. What then is the alternative? It must be that our completed physics captures only some range of properties of the world of appearance. Other beings' completed science should capture the rest, or at least part of the rest. Only then the idea of our striving for one real maximal system seems to have escaped us: our systematization of the world is at best maximal only for what is available to us, not maximal *haplōs*. Then again, we cannot surely rule out the possibility that there may be an even more all-embracing theoretical structure that incorporates both what is given to us and what is envisaged as given to others, though any such maximal system would presumably demand to be captured in a vocabulary that no single party can command.[21] In that situation, it might be right to say, rather despondently, that we must assume that our own 'completed' physics is not what fixes the point of absolute objectivity *even for what is accessible to us*. Would that then deprive our claims about our own world of pretension to truth, defined, as that pretension is, in terms of fully objective judgement? An answer that invites exploration on Kant's behalf is that since our own eventually completed science will be as systematic as is possible for us, it would be attractive to suppose that its findings would be incorporated in the wider system, the hyper-GUT that lies beyond our power to formulate. In that case, even if we came to acknowledge that fully objective validity in judgement lay beyond us, limited now not just in its extent, but in its very nature as well, our experiential and inferential judgements about appearances would none the less retain their claim to truth by being grounded on 'the object' within a fully objective hyper-GUT that it would be beyond the reach of our understanding to articulate.

The gist of these last reflections, then, is this. Were Kant to accept the deflationary argument about the impossibility of other sorts of receptive experience than our own, his positive metaphysic of experience, his Empirical Realism, would be anti-realist while, of course, his metaphysics of the world, his negative Transcendental Idealism, is starkly realist in nature. That is, with respect to appearances, there is no room for in-principle-verification-transcendent truth, and so all empirical reality lies theoretically open to us. By contrast, the world in itself necessarily transcends all investigation of its intrinsic nature. However, if that familiar move is declined, in line with the text, Kant will then find himself unable to rule out the possibility of aspects of appearance that constitutionally elude us. But it may be that they are still not theoretically verification-transcendent. It is just that verification would have to be carried out directly and inferentially by creatures with other powers than those we have. On the other hand, and pushing speculation even further than Kant himself does, were he to suppose that the idea of full objective validity ultimately requires there being a unified hyper-GUT or hyper-TOE that embraces all matters empirical whatever, yet which constitutionally eludes any specific kind of receptivity-dependent subject, then the metaphysic of the world of appearance would turn out to be no less realist than that of the world in itself. Our consequently limited idea of objective validity, no longer just limited in extent, but limited in nature too, would leave us viewing our beliefs and those of our alien fellows as being better than approximately true only if we had some reason to suppose our own local GUTs were comfortably nested in the grander, ineffable and inscrutable hyper-GUT. Along which of these paths we ought to journey is not something that the *Critique* reveals.

The last part of this discussion has been about objective validity of our experience and its limits. It has not touched on our right to suppose that our grasp of the world of appearances is truly cognitive, but only on conditions that need to be satisfied if it is to be so. Kant's way of assuring us on the latter score and of surmounting the difficulties faced here by his predecessors is something to which we may now turn.

6

Cognitive Rewards:
The Refutation of Idealism,
the Self and Others

Although the main focus of Kant's interest has been on our potential grasp of the world around us in perceptual experience, his ultimate goal is to provide assurance that knowledge of the world of appearance is available to us even to the depths of space and time. This is illustrated by his acceptance of Newtonian claims about the hyperbolic career of comets that appear only intermittently to our view (A663/B691).[1] Here we have an explicit instance of Kant claiming knowledge extending far beyond present perception and of our dependence on inference in obtaining it. Evidently, this is bound to puzzle the reader, because one of the main reasons Kant had for dissatisfaction with earlier attempts to provide a sound basis for our beliefs about the surrounding world was precisely that they relied on inference. Specifically in the case of Descartes and Locke, those attempted inferences were hopeless. So, if the one all-embracing nature which we are bound to construct for ourselves in bringing cognitive order to what would otherwise be a buzzing confusion of stimuli can only be achieved by relying on speculative inferences, the question must be how Kant is to avoid falling victim to his very own implicit polemic. Moreover, if he succeeds at this point, won't that then encourage one to suppose that inferential roads to the in-itself are also on the cards?

To meet this double challenge Kant inserts a short passage (B274–9) into the Postulates of Empirical Thought, that is, those Principles of Pure Understanding generated by the three categories of Modality, that he labels 'Refutation of Idealism'. This is a widely admired proof that we have immediate perceptual knowledge of the external world which is neither open to the sort of doubt Descartes had raised a century and a half earlier, nor achieved at the cost of treating the concept *matter* as nonsensical in the way Berkeley had supposed. The Refutation is often taken out of context, though; and as we read it, we should remember that what is going on is more than anything else a prelude to affirming that inferential conclusions reaching beyond what is available to us in experience are perfectly legitimate and, indeed, transcendentally necessary if the demands of the unity of apperception are to be fully satisfied.

The key to the puzzle, as Kant sees it, is that we have to persuade ourselves that we have immediate *non-inferential* awareness of external objects in space, and that as long as that is secured, inference to empirical material lying beyond perception will in principle be unobjectionable. What Kant thought went wrong in the case of Descartes and Locke was that they had thought immediate awareness was only of their own mental states, and they had wrongly presumed that we need to employ inference to move beyond that even to the external objects closest to us, even to our own bodies. Like them, Berkeley had made the same choice of starting point, and only avoided the need to rely on inferences, which he well recognized to be untenable, by adopting the catastrophic expedient of identifying objects in external world, our bodies among them, with our own inner states, our ideas. All three philosophers count as *idealists* in Kant's sense because, in different ways, they are unable to make good our claims to have proper knowledge of the material world. Descartes and Locke are *problematic* idealists because while they did not doubt the existence of the extended world, the inferences they relied on to convert their firm belief into knowledge were unsustainable; Berkeley is a *dogmatic* idealist on account of his supposing that there could be no such independently existing extended world anyway, hence nothing material for us to have knowledge of. In Kant's language 'idealism' is often synonymous with 'scepticism', which is a usage that fits his own 'Transcendental Idealism' well enough, since once that is distinguished from Empirical Realism, it affirms only that we can have no knowledge of the world that transcends (underlies, grounds) appearances. That is a scepticism which is obligatory for Kant, though it does not extend to the world of appearances, of which we do presumably have both immediate perceptual and well-grounded inferential knowledge. To show this is the task of the Refutation. It is, Kant tells us, 'a strict and . . . the only possible proof of the objective reality of outer intuition' (Bxxxix fn.).

The thesis of the Refutation is that 'The mere, but empirically determined, consciousness of my own existence proves the existence of objects in space outside me' (B275). The structure of the argument to that conclusion is straightforward enough. For Kant, just as for Descartes and his successors, there was no doubt that we have knowledge of our own mental states. Examples no one would contest would be: 'I have had a splitting headache all morning'; 'I remember the smell of tarred cricket-netting last summer'; and Descartes' own famous: 'I am entertaining the proposition "I am, I exist" '. What such examples have in common is that the subject of these mental states either implicitly or explicitly situates his possession of those mental states in time, as lasting all morning, as occurring at this very moment, and so on.[2] Hence, as a first premise, we have, rather cumbersomely expressed, 'I am conscious of my own existence as determined in time.'

Such are prime and undisputed instances of secure cognition. Now, Kant takes it that the First Analogy has already established that our dependence on the form of inner sense, time, must have an experiential manifestation, and that temporal duration ('all morning') and determinate temporal position ('now', 'last summer', etc.) can only be manifest though what is given us in space. As he puts it in the Refutation's second premise, and harking back to the First Analogy, 'All determination in time presupposes something permanent in perception.' With this in hand, he proceeds to argue that the permanent in question cannot itself be a perceptual state of my own for the reason that all my perceptual states are representations that take place at particular times. Adjusting the body of the B275 text in the Preface to the later edition at Bxxxix, Kant says that, being merely representations that change from time to time, they 'require a permanent distinct from them in relation to which their change, and so my existence in the time wherein they change, may be determined'. So, my passing headache can be dated and related temporally to other inner states of mine such as my remembering the smell of tarred netting earlier that same morning. For that to be possible, the very time in which these inner states occurred has to be introduced. That, in turn, can only be done through my experiential access to an outer world. It is that, and that alone, which enables me to be self-consciously aware of my inner states at all.

The philosopher who Kant imagines accepting that his inner states might be dated in relation to some inner representation of a persisting state might be Hume (although Kant does not say so), for in the Appendix to the *Treatise* Hume had envisaged that his puzzlement about the nature and existence of the self might be solved if there were either some 'real connection' among our mental states or else some persisting and unchanging impression to which the others were related. Setting aside the obscure 'real connection' and concentrating on the hypothetical persisting inner state, we can see Kant objecting that its persistence can only be its enduring for a determinate period of time, say from 1745 to 1748, and that idea of temporal extension itself has to be legitimately introduced, which requires the perception of external objects in space. Hume, or his disciples, might suppose that the perception of such objects could be accepted as long as this was understood to mean no more than that we would have to have *impressions* as of such things, but that is just what Kant is refusing to allow. Such impressions are themselves states of the subject that occur at particular times and last for determinate lengths of time, and so can only be introduced in our confrontation with real persisting objects in space, not just impressions of such things.

In this way Kant takes it he has overcome *problematic* idealism because he has shown any awareness of our inner states presupposes that we have unproblematic, non-inferential awareness of the outer world. And *dogmatic* scepticism is refuted just because awareness of the permanent in perception that is presupposed by awareness of our mental states (*scilicet*, ideas) can only be of material things (material substance(s)). This last point, on which everything turns, is so important for Kant's general philosophy of time and nature that his own elaboration of it a little later on demands notice.

The central idea goes back to Kant's conception of the manifold that we are originally given in intuition, just the buzzing, unordered sensory stimuli. They have to be ordered in time, and as that ordering has to be manifest in our experience it requires that we synthesize the manifold through the categories of substance and causality and in accordance with the mathematical and dynamical Principles.[3] Introducing the idea of lasting time into experience requires that I have the idea of the passage of time, and temporal passage can only be manifest in the perception of change, the same thing now being in one state and then a little later in a different, opposed state. If there is to be an answer to the question how much later it was that something came to be *G* after having previously been *F*, there has to be a way of measuring time, and that can only be through the observation of movement in space, as, say, the movement of the large hand of a clock over 15 minutes through the arc from VI to IX. As Kant puts it at B292, 'The presence of the point in different locations (as a sequence of opposite determinations) is what alone first yields to us an intuition of alteration'. He goes on: 'For in order that we may afterwards make inner intuition likewise thinkable, we must represent time (the form of inner sense) figuratively as a line, and the inner alteration through the drawing of this line (motion), and so in this manner by means of outer intuition make comprehensible the successive existence of ourselves in different states.' Hence the insistence that experience present us with material things, since only they can be space-occupiers.

Kant supplements the dense argument of the Refutation by adding three Notes (B276–9), effectively mopping up objections of one kind or another that he foresees a critic raising. Of these the first and the third are of particular interest. The first of them stresses the *immediacy* of our perception of spatial objects: 'In the above proof it has been shown that outer experience is really immediate, and that only by means of it is inner experience – not indeed the consciousness of my own existence, but the determination of it in time – possible.' And in a footnote flagging the word 'immediate' Kant undertakes to show that it would not be possible to understand the immediate consciousness we have of outer things as being merely given to 'an outer imagination', as, say, in dreams, and not to an outer sense proper. The argument here introduces something new. It is that if we are to view something as outer, and so present it to sense in intuition, which is what we do in synthesizing all our perceptual experience (see especially A100–2), we need first to be presented with something passively and receptively. That is what the active faculty needs if it is to have something to work on. But as we here try to envisage doing without an outer sense, we deprive ourselves of the very thing that we need if we are to use understanding spontaneously and actively. As Kant puts it, 'should we merely be imagining an outer sense, the faculty of intuition, which is to be determined by the faculty of imagination, would itself be annulled' (B277).[4]

The third Note warns the reader that the Refutation does not aim to show that just any apparent perception of objects in space must be a presentation to sense of a really existent object. Dreams and illusions testify to the falsity of any such thought (B278). So, to the Cartesian doubter of the *First Meditation* who says of any intuition that it might just be a dream, Kant can say that that is indeed so, but that that is entirely consistent with the thought that at least some intuitions must be veridical.[5] At least the awareness of outer things through outer representations must be possible. This Kant puts by saying that dreams and illusion merely reproduce previous outer perceptions which themselves 'are possible only through the reality of outer objects' (B278).

It would be a mistake to think that at the end of the Principles we are left in the position of knowing that some of our perceptual experiences must be veridical but no means of knowing which. If that were so, the point of the Refutation would be missed, since it seeks to show that we can acquire knowledge by inference that is not directly verifiable in perception. If we never knew which of our seemingly outer intuitions were veridical, we would never know when we had conducted empirical inference on a sound basis. Its utility in expanding our knowledge beyond present perception would then lapse.

In fact Kant has very little to say about the particular case, though at B279 he does observe that '[w]hether this or that supposed experience be not purely imaginary, must be ascertained from its special determinations, and through its congruence with the criteria of all real experience'. If we take this together with the discussion at the end of the last chapter, it should be clear what Kant has in mind. What is in question here is knowledge, not truth, so what we want is a view of evidential support for belief that when truth is given, knowledge results.[6] Within Kant's form of empirical realism, strong evidential support for a belief about some outer intuition will be supplied jointly by two things. First, our representations must appear to conform with the criteria we have adopted in introducing the concepts in terms of which the belief is articulated. Then, secondly, the belief in question needs to fit smoothly into the unified structure of the natural world which the proper use of our understanding obliges us to construct. If at these two points our belief resists challenge we shall have every reason to think it true, and then, provided that it is true, what we believe, we know.[7/8]

It was preoccupation with Hume's problem about the external world that aroused Kant from his dogmatic slumbers (*Prolegomena*, Introduction), so how does he suppose the Refutation helps him to deal with that? For Hume, objects in the world are vulgarly thought of as possessing independence of the mind, as existing at some distance from the subject and as continuing to exist when not perceived. It would be easy to suppose that the Kantian treatment of external objects as appearances, just as one's own states, fails to meet these requirements too, which are after all no more than requirements of common sense. In response, Kant must say that this is a misperception of his suggestion. Appearances (*Erscheinungen*), I have already insisted, are not the same as apprehensions (*Apprehensionen*) or perceptions (*Wahrnehmungen*), and we must not allow Kant's occasionally saying that bodies are merely representations in us, as, for instance, he does at A370, to persuade us otherwise. That is an unhappy mis-statement his position, and one that is generally removed in the B edition. Appearances are indeed objects, only objects as they are liable to appear to us, and it is only in that sense that they can be called 'merely representations in us'. So what exists when I turn off the light after observing the red pill-box on my bedroom chest of drawers is, and remains, a red pill-box, for that is the appearance that is disposed to present itself to me as a red pill-box when I come to attend to it once again in daylight. It is at a distance from me, because it is something that, when I attend to it, will be perceived as being at such and such a place in my bedroom. Similarly for independence. If I were to cease to exist, the pill-box would nevertheless remain. Of course, if the box were sealed in some impenetrable vault, it would cease to appear to anyone, it would not display itself in space and time, but it would still be correct to say that it existed in space and time, and hence still be an appearance, just because it would still be disposed to affect people in that way if there were any around to observe it. That thought suffices to secure the box's independence, while maintaining that the objects known to us are only appearances and not things in themselves. 'Appearances that do not appear' does at first sound oxymoronic. Understood in this Kantian way, however, it is not.[9]

Kant can still allow that it is a logical possibility that any of our empirical beliefs should be false, but if that were to be put to him he should also stress, as Descartes had done earlier,[10] that that gives us no serious and well-meditated reason to doubt them. It is just a recognition that empirical belief is fallible, and no one should find in that anything to concern them. Confronted with the persistent sceptic worrying about the reliability of our outer experience, Kant can say that once the two principal conditions on reasonable belief mentioned above are satisfied, the onus is on the querulous doubter to make out that something is amiss. Until he can do that our (fallible) claim to know what the world is like on the basis of perceptual experience will stand.

In the *Essay*, at IV.xi.9, Locke expresses confidence that he can know that something in the world beyond the mind is responsible for our perceptions, but that confidence wanes when we move away from that and speculate whether that something exists beyond the present moment, or whether it was the same thing as was responsible for similar earlier perceptual experiences. Kant does not address the question directly, but on his way to securing more daring inferential conclusions down the line, he can say that once we have established that present perception presents us immediately with persisting external things, we can legitimately infer that what we witnessed a little while ago will have existed before we saw it, and will continue to do so in the absence of destructive forces.[11] Likewise, given the kind of stable world the Principles of Understanding ensure we build up, that must also make it possible for us to answer questions about identity of objects perceived at different times by legitimate inferential means. So the Refutation serves to provide a base for enlarging our cognitive grasp of the world beyond what is immediately given to us in perception in just the way that common sense takes for granted.

What then about more speculative theoretical and scientific beliefs acquired by inference from perceptual or experimental evidence? Kant mentions two specific cases where he thinks our claim knowledge is uncontroversial. The first, immediately preceding the Refutation at A226/B273, is where, from observation of the behaviour of iron filings, we infer to the existence of 'a magnetic matter pervading all bodies, although the constitution of our bodies cuts us off from all immediate perception of this medium'. In this case, there is no reason to doubt the accuracy of the initial observation. The causal determinism which requires that there be an explanation for the filings' behaviour in the world of appearance is in order from the Second Analogy, and Kant takes it that the hypothesis of a magnetic medium is in accord with the unifying scientific principles which allow us to build up our conception of a single natural world. So he takes it that the inference is warranted and can be taken as an authentic case of knowledge.

As it happens, we now know that the mechanical system that Kant adopted, in the wake of Descartes and Newton, was flawed. Forces act not only mechanically, but also at a distance, and neither gravity nor electro-magnetic force require a medium to be effective. So in this case a sceptical doubter of Kant's inferential belief would have been able to show that one of the conditions that he thought good inference has to meet to yield genuine knowledge was not met. That would have been an embarrassment to Kant in the matter of the iron filings, but it would not have undermined his general story about sound theoretical inference.

The other notable case, already encountered, is that of inference from the observation of short-period comets passing through the solar system to the hyperbolic nature of their orbits, which is something 'such as experience could never confirm' (B691). The same principles as before determine whether the inference is legitimate, and whether it allows us to claim knowledge. In this case, while today we have the ability to make far more precise claims about the comets than was possible in Kant's day, for the rather imprecise claim that he had in mind his own conditions for inferential soundness appear to be met, and so yield knowledge of a kind about appearances which are not open to direct scrutiny.

The inclusion of observationally unconfirmable inferential knowledge should not be taken to threaten Kant's claim that we only have access to the phenomenal world (the world of appearance). Of course, that could suggest that everything we know about must be able to appear in perception, and in his discussion of the medium of magnetism Kant does say that it is merely due to the grossness of our senses that this does not occur. But obviously, there are cases in which that suggestion is not at all plausible and Kant would be well advised not to insist on the point. To take one example, our inferential knowledge of the very small cannot be subjected to any such constraint, since we humans could not possibly have senses of the requisite acuity, and beneath a certain threshold nor could any other living organism. To convince oneself of that, we need only reflect on knowledge we now have about the state of the cosmos in its first few moments, or the knowledge we now take ourselves to have of the universe's eventual collapse in some Big Crunch to see the irrelevance of supposing ourselves hypothetically to enjoy more impressive powers of sensory discrimination.[12]

A question that needs to be answered is how we can think of extending the world of appearance so far by inference without thereby assimilating the in-itself to it. One suggestion might be to say that 'appearance' extends to anything that lies within the world that is given to us in perception, and it sounds in good enough harmony with Kant's views. Only the difficulty is to know exactly how one should rebut the objection that the world-in-itself lies in that same world, since, on the present interpretation of Kant, in perception it is ultimately things in themselves that appear to us in this way or that. However that may be, one will preserve Kantian reticence at this point well enough by stressing that the cosmic inferences he is concerned with all are about the world that is bound by space and time, and hence still thought of through the exercise of sense and understanding from the restricted human point of view. That should be enough to preserve continuity with the initial conception we have of 'appearance' and enable us to exclude from its extension the result of any inferential allusions to the in-itself conducted under the aegis of pure reason.[13]

* * *

In an earlier chapter I undertook to say something about Kant's position on the self. Naturally enough, in the wake of others, Kant does not suppose that there is any problem about knowledge of our own mental states, in particular of how our experience of the world is presented to us in inner sense. He has little more than a passing remark to make about the issue of Other Minds, and he employs his 'dualism' to assert inevitable ignorance about the nature of the self. These matters surface only briefly in the Paralogisms, that part of the Dialectic that is concerned with the impossibility of rational, i.e. non-empirical, psychology, and then primarily in the A edition. In the B edition the positive treatment of the topic almost completely fades away. So, it might look as if it would be a waste of time to pause over Kant's positive reflections in this area. That, however, would be a mistake. The reason is that if we apply the new way of thinking that the B edition offers us about the relation of the noumenal and the phenomenal and apply Kant's Empirical Realism consistently, we come upon results that are very surprising indeed. To get to those results we need to start off from what we are told in A.

At A342/B400 Kant claims that ' "I" designates two kinds of objects – "I" as thinking, am an object of inner sense, and am called "soul". That which is an object of the outer senses is called "body".'[14] Because what appears is so different in the two cases, we cannot say that empirically we have to do with a single entity, and Kant insists that it is at most a possibility that the 'transcendental object' underlying these different appearances could be one and the same (A358). Here he is clearly using 'transcendental object' to mean the thing-in-itself which affects us in both inner and outer sense. This is even clearer at A346/B304, where Kant speaks of whatever the 'I, he or it' is and, thinking of it from the inner perspective, declares that the 'transcendental subject' is unknown to us except through the thoughts, feeling and so on that it has. It is as though when I think about what is given to me in outer sense, I am aware of empirical substances, among them men and women, but seemingly, in rather a Cartesian vein, only as bodies that are properly understood in mechanical terms. Their movements are at best 'signs' of some inner life.

At A359, we come across an intriguing suggestion.

> I may further assume that the substance which, in relation to our outer sense possesses extension is in itself the possessor of thoughts, and that these thoughts can by means of its own inner sense be consciously represented. In this way, what in one relation is entitled corporeal would in another relation be at the same time a thinking being, whose thoughts we cannot intuit, though we can intuit their signs in the field of appearance. Accordingly the thesis that only souls think, would have to be given up; and we should have to fall back on the common expression that men think, that is, that the very same being, which as outer appearance, is extended, is (in itself) internally a subject, and is not composite, but is simple and thinks.

The idea Kant is still pursuing in this passage seems to be that the thinking self that corresponds to the body which is given in outer sense, in particular in the cases when we have to do with others, is a noumenal subject, and that we use the word 'man' to designate not so much two objects but one, a phenomenal subject that manifests itself to outer sense as a body whose behaviour is a sign of an inner life which each of us, in our own case, but in no other, is aware of directly through inner sense.

However, these interesting sentences are complicated by turning up in a context in which Kant is clearly considering the in-itself, and what is entirely missing from my paraphrase is the salient thought that the mental states of which we are aware in inner sense in default of any consciously presented subject have to be provided with a noumenal one. There is clear tension here, because once the noumenal subject is introduced, it is hard to align with Kant's observing that we fall back on the common way of expressing ourselves and saying that men think.

Is there anything to be done here within the kind of empirical realism that Kant endorses? The answer is surely 'Yes', providing that we move stepwise, progressively. The first thing to notice is that the category we are concerned with is not the category merely of substance, but, to give it its full title, that of substance-and-inherence. What we are given in inner sense, our own thoughts, are states of ourselves, and it would seem to be almost obligatory for Kant to say that as the category is applied in time, we need to find an *empirical* subject for those empirical states to be states of.

Sometimes it seems plain beyond dispute that what we are aware of in inner sense are our own bodies. I have had a splitting headache all morning; I sense you soothing my fevered brow; you feel yourself being spun round on the Wall of Death. In cases such as these it is entirely natural to suppose that what is immediately accessible to one person in inner sense is equally immediately available to another in outer sense. Just as you feel yourself whizzing round pinned to the wall by centrifugal force, so, standing outside the pit, I see you pinned there whizzing round. When a person suffers from toothache, Kant would have every reason to say that it is a state of his teeth that presents itself to him in the unpleasant way that most adults know from the inside, a state of the teeth that is as immediately open to the dentist's inspection in outer sense as it is to his patient from the inside.

Admittedly, these examples are not prime cases of inner *thought*, which is what Kant is primarily focused on, but they can all serve well as instances of the initial premise of the Refutation: 'I am aware of myself as determined in time'. We shall come to the issue of thought shortly. Now, it might be supposed that even this initial step is objectionable on the ground that Kant seems to think that inner sense necessarily has a subject that outer sense does not, and vice versa, so that whenever I am aware of my body, it must be the case that I am aware of it in outer sense. However, in the first place, he never says this, and secondly, the examples just used point conclusively to the falsity of the idea. Let us not foist it onto him if it can be helped.[15]

Let us say then that sometimes in inner sense we are aware of our own bodies from within presenting themselves to us as being in this state or that. We can allow without embarrassment that the way those states present themselves to us are very largely different from the way they present themselves to other people: I feel my apoplectic rage burning within, you see my rage in my bearing and contorted face, but that is no reason for us to say that we aren't both sensitive to the same thing, the same state of my body. And even then, it is a contingent matter that what I am aware of in inner sense, I am not also aware of in outer sense. Even if it's a necessary truth that my surgeon cannot feel my pain, I can observe my swollen brain pressing on the nerves as well as he can, providing only that I have access to the same instruments as he does. The crucial difference on which we need to concentrate is between two different ways of accessing the same thing, rather than that between different people's access to that same thing.

In some cases at least it seems right to say that there is nothing to stop Kant from saying that what is presented to me in inner sense is the very same thing as is presented to an observer in outer sense (where that observer can be myself). In these cases we can say the subject of the inner states is the man, and without any implication that it is some remote and elusive 'transcendental subject'. If we were indeed forced to go transcendental, as Kant supposes, the transcendental subject will be the same thing as the transcendental object, if there has to be one. For if the empirical object that I am presented with in way W in inner sense is the empirical object presented to your outward sense in way W' then the real, transcendental subject underlying what is presented to me cannot be other than the real, transcendental object underlying what is presented to you. But that just by the way.

What moves Kant to introduce the unknown (transcendental) subject is that in most cases of self-awareness we are not aware of anything other than our mental states. There seems to be no self given to us as the subject of those states, or so Hume had taught. I feel philosophical puzzlement, but not the self who is puzzled. I feel fear, but without being presented with a self whose fear I feel. And it seems that because a state has to be a state of some subject, Kant is moved at this point to introduce the in-itself one, a kind of obligatory dummy to be supplied when an empirical subject cannot be located.

At this point let us notice two things about our experience through *outer* sense. First, sometimes we are aware of some state of a thing, without being aware of the thing itself. So, going by that familiar smell, I can say the wretched dog has been in the sitting-room again. Of greater relevance to the issue at hand, I can also in outer sense be aware of some state of an object, yet be ignorant of what object I have to do with. So a visitor can wonder what it is that smells just like that. In neither case would Kant suppose himself to be under any pressure to say that the elusive subject is the dog in-itself. Instead he can say that my sensitivity to the state of the dog didn't involve the immediate presence in my experience of the dog; and he can also say that we can often synthesize experience in such a way that we recognize states to be of something empirical but which my present evidence leaves indeterminate for me. Only later on does my visitor discover that the smell that beset him was the smell of the dog.

Returning now to the topic of *inner* sense and the self: suppose we take it for granted, as Kant seems to have done, that the only things that are given to me in inner sense are states of the self or my own body and its states, and suppose also that it is allowed that wherever there is awareness of a thing's states there has to be some empirical subject of those states. Then a very inviting inference would be that what it is that possesses the thoughts and experiences that I have must be the one thing that does present itself to me in inner sense on occasion, to wit my very own body. So, for example, when I feel myself struggling with some philosophical puzzlement (like this one) I suggest it would be open to Kant to say that I am aware of a certain state of my own body (which is what is me, or my self) from within. That bodily state presents itself to me in the guise of philosophical puzzlement, and the subject of that puzzlement is the very same as the subject of the bodily state, my body, me, my very self.

One thing that earlier philosophers, Kant among them maybe, would have found unacceptable about this, is that their mechanical conception of the body seems to leave no room for thought. Thought cannot be reduced to the mechanical grinding of wheels and levers, an idea clearly expressed by Leibniz at *Monadology* §17.[16] And in the mechanically conceived world, there is nothing other than such grinding, so thought appears to have no place there at all. However, what is wrong with this reflection is to infer that because the body is composed entirely of mechanically related parts, that fixes how the arrangements of those parts are registered by the body itself. Of course, it is natural to suppose that they must in some way or other, say in observation from an external vantage point, be registered as mechanically moving parts. Yet that does not exclude their also being registered in some other way, as in the case of the splitting headache, when the registration is not from an external vantage point, but from the point of view of Leibniz's suffering watermill itself, the body monitoring its own internal states.

From the passage quoted above we see that Kant proposes to regard what is observed from without as *a sign* of what is going on within, possibly a sign of some other state of the same noumenal subject, where the sign is the basis of legitimate inference. This must be unsatisfactory, since there is no basis whatever for me to suppose that what in my case are bodily states regularly correlated with given states of my mind or soul are, when observed in others, regularly correlated with mental states of theirs. As Kant asks in other contexts: Where is the necessity that makes any such association a necessary rule, and without which the inference would be groundless? Having no access to the inner lives of others, what legitimacy could there be in treating the behaviour of outwardly observed creatures as signs of anything? There seems to be no answer.

But with the groundwork laid, and the thought in place that the empirical subject of my thoughts can be nothing other than my body, it does become available to Kant to suppose that in outer sense we are not aware only of signs of people's inner lives, but on occasion of the very states that in their inner lives they are aware of as thoughts. Suppose that in a chess match you, White, are threatened by a bishop–knight fork in a couple of moves, and can see that. You spend a little time working out how to forestall the threat and think through your next moves and those open to your opponent, Black. I, an onlooker alert to Black's threat, observe your thinking out your defensive strategy through the immediate awareness I have of the bodily behaviour which you are inwardly aware of as those defensive thoughts you are thinking.[17] (Of course, there is plenty of room for inference to fail here, but as in the case of the external world, inference will be justifiable enough as long as if sometimes I have immediate access to what you are aware of inwardly in what is given to me outwardly.)

I have said that these are lines of thought open to Kant within the framework of his Empirical Realism. They are emphatically not views he actually expresses. None the less, we can ask how sympathetic he might have been to them if he had thought it interesting to take up the positive thoughts about the self in the B edition, from which it has almost entirely disappeared. The differences between A ands B that have emerged as significant have been twofold. First there is the suppression of the two-world view of the relation between phenomena and noumena. Then there is its replacement by a two-aspect view of the same thing (one aspect of which is not available to us).[18] For present purposes it is the second of these moves which is suggestive, for while Kant clings to the idea that we have no access to the noumenal, the general idea of there being two different views on the same thing is not restricted to the topic phenomena/noumena and does not of itself imply that wherever it is in place only one aspect of the phenomenal states involved should be available, either ever, or to a particular individual, or in particular cases. So, instead of viewing the thinking self and the bodily self as two distinct 'I's as he does at A342/B400, it would be a natural enough line to explore that the inner view and the outer view are different ways in which the same subject presents itself to view. And, as we have seen, since empirically given states require empirically given subjects, what presents itself to view must be a physical thing in both cases, the man, as Kant says, not a body in one case, and a soul in the other. Indeed, moving away from the soul altogether, Kant says at B415 that the permanence of the soul during life is, of course, evident *per se*, since the thinking being (a man) is itself likewise an object of the outer senses, 'likewise' meaning, surely, just as it is an object of inner sense. Here we seem to have outright endorsement of the suggestion I am making on Kant's behalf, even if in a very passing way.

In the light of the move away from the dualistic two-worlds doctrine, Kant's form of mind–body dualism within the empirical world can be eased out. The benefits of doing so are enormous, as can be seen from the ways that then open up for Kant to answer traditionally vexing questions: What is the self? Available answer: for each of us, a particular living human body, the body each of us refers to as 'I'. Why think there are other persons apart from myself? Answer: because there are bodies observably like mine. How am I justified in ascribing mental states to them? Answer: because in some cases I am aware of the same sorts of bodily states in them as I am aware of in my own case, which states present themselves to me from the inside as mental. If I can sometimes be aware of such states in others immediately, then that will underwrite the possibility of legitimate inference to their mental life in other cases. Can we be immortal? Answer: the self can last only as long as the living body, being the living body. How are the mind and body united? Answer: If this is really a question about the relation between two kinds of state, they are not states of two kinds. They are both bodily states, but the mental is that class of bodily states that present themselves to us from within in the guise of thought, experience, feeling and so on. Finally, is there a primitive certainty that we have about our own mental states? Answer: as states of the body, they ultimately have to be fitted into the one nature that the Principles of Understanding claim is founded on the unity of apperception. So we must be ready to recast our ways of thinking about ourselves should we need to in the light of systematic scientific advance. This doesn't imply that we are wrong in the ways we think about ourselves, but only that we cannot exclude the possibility that we shall need to readjust ingrained habits of thought in the pursuit of finer and fuller understanding of our world and the place we have in it.

Quite apart from these matters there is one other signal benefit to the Kantian system that this proposal brings with it. It is that it gives Kant a way of unifying the time of inner and outer sense. As we started off, the manifold was apprehended in time and the challenge was to fashion a world of objects that persisted and were either co-existent or successive. To date, the focus of attention has been exclusively the temporality of outer sense, and that leaves open the question how my awareness inwardly of myself as determined in time fits into the same time series as that of objects given to me in outer sense. The answer has to be because the subject of my awareness is itself located in the same arena as those objects of outer sense, and it is only when we are able to identify that subject as a body that this answer becomes available. If there is no empirical self and only its noumenal dummy, the unity of time which has all along been taken for granted will remain an insoluble mystery.

Then, too, we have an answer to questions Kant does not ask but which his frequent appeal to the transcendental unity of apperception makes salient. What is it for the self to persist through time? When are temporally distinct judgements to the effect that I think or experience such and such judgements of the same subject? The absence of an empirical subject leaves the question without an answer, and appeal to an inscrutable noumenal subject leaves the answer utterly obscure. By contrast, if the thinking subject is the body, the answer is evident. Identity of the self through time is provided by persistence of the body (suitably alive and alert) and two distinct exercises of Descartes' *cogito* will testify to the existence of one self rather than two if and only if it is the same body that conducts the exercise on both occasions.

Incorporating these thoughts about the self into Kant's general philosophy enables us to understand how knowledge concerning the self and its states is as much subject to the overarching methodological requirements as knowledge of the outer world. We saw how that methodology led us to think of appearances that were understood as entities subject to laws of conservation, reciprocal causation and inertia. It is by connecting the self and its states to the body that it finds its place in this laboriously unified construction of the world. By contrast, the Cartesian picture of the self ensures that it resists incorporation in the wider structure of the material world, and thus sets up a fundamental obstacle to the success of the scientific revolution that Descartes himself had initiated. Once self and body are properly unified, Kant need fear no such danger, and he can escape that ominous threat without supposing that the physical sciences must be able to extend their reach to the ways in which the human body represents itself and its own states from the inside.

* * *

At the start of the chapter I raised the question whether the legitimization of theoretical inference as a way of extending our cognitive grasp of the world might not lead to unwelcome consequences for Kant's own form of idealism. So, for instance, it now appears to be a straightforward empirical claim that we know there to be things-in-themselves, or noumena in the negative sense (things in so far as they are not objects of our sensible intuition (B307)), a claim that is supported by the same kind of considerations as had led Descartes and Locke to suppose that there were bodies lurking behind the veil of perception they aspired to penetrate. In Kant's case, we move from the thought that sensibility is passive and receptive and infer that there must be something that makes its impact on the senses. This is really what lies behind the claim at A249: 'Now we must bear in mind that the concept of appearances, as limited by the Transcendental Aesthetic, already of itself establishes the objective reality of noumena, and justifies the division of objects into *phaenomena and noumena*', which would otherwise amount to little more than the seemingly analytic claim that appearances must be appearances of something, and which yields no existential conclusion. Here, by contrast, just as was the case with Descartes and Locke, as we reflect on the nature of our receptivity, we are struck by the recalcitrance of intuition to the will, and are invited to accept an existential claim because of its explanatory power.[19]

Kant would not be alarmed by this observation. The empirical introduction of noumena is harmless enough as long as we don't expect to be able to acquire *determinate* knowledge about such things and as long as we recognize that this in no way prejudices our cognitive access to the world of appearance. We may even suppose that if they make their impact on the senses and on each other, these relational matters must themselves depend on some intrinsic features of these noumenal things. So, again, we infer abductively that there must be features of the noumenal things we are sensitive to in perception yet which are impenetrable to us either by direct inspection, or by theoretical inference. And that Kant will say is no more than the doctrine of Transcendental Idealism itself. As long as we are clear that all the *determinate* knowledge we have of the world is a reflection of the ways in which the mind colours the way the world appears to us both receptively and in our spontaneous synthesis of passively received sensory input, the introduction of noumena is entirely benign. The mistake of Descartes and of Locke was to suppose that the veil of perception was to some extent permeable (more so in Descartes' case than in Locke's), and further to suppose that unless it were so, much empirical knowledge would lie beyond our reach.

At first blush, of course, talk of the inscrutable world in-itself sounds like metaphysical tosh of the kind that Kant would be among the first to abjure. That impression is reinforced in the A edition by his speaking of phenomena and noumena making up two distinct worlds (to say nothing of the specious argument from the concept of appearance). However, when, in B, the two-world view gives way to the two-aspect way of thinking, what would be mysterious is not the abductively inferred existence of noumena and their intrinsic properties, but their absence. Without them, what sense could we make of our experience at all when that is understood as Kant presents it? That mystery he is happy to spare us.

7

Appreciation

Newton liked to say that that he was only able to see as far as he did by standing on the shoulders of giants. That thought could well have been echoed by Kant. In this last chapter, I outline ways in which his Empirical Realism takes him beyond his predecessors, and then say something about the way in which he relied on what they passed on to him even while their teachings were left behind. Finally, I suggest reasons there may be for distancing ourselves from Kant's vision of the world and, at the very end, ask what alternative is left open.

First and foremost, the Kantian system provides a clear non-theologically grounded route to empirical knowledge of an independently existing world. Our knowledge covers what is given to us directly in present perception, and so allows Kant to equate experience with knowledge. Further, our cognitive grasp of the world extends for Kant, as it did not for Locke, to what is available to perception but is not actually perceived, as when I know from memory what lies on the far side of a closed door. This is fundamentally secured through the legitimization of induction and abduction as it falls out of the Principles. Then, thirdly, knowledge extends to what is not even available to observation through the construction of coherent theory and its implications for our understanding of what perceptual experience does reveal. In each of these three ways Kant is able to step way beyond his predecessors, and he would say this is the just reward of his Copernican turn. In addition, I have suggested, his philosophy promises a way of integrating what is given in inner sense with what is available to outer sense, and, although Kant makes no boast about this, the promise of such unification is another impressive addition to his quiver.

Allowing the world of appearance to present itself to us directly in perception, Kant easily side-steps the problem of penetrating the veil of perception, which Descartes and Locke had both faced only without understanding how to deal with it. Then, because the world of appearance is fully open to inspection and to fruitful empirical investigation, Kant is immune to Hume's sceptical puzzle deriving from his assessment of that veil as being logically impenetrable. Nevertheless, we can say that there does still remain a veil for Kant, and one that is indeed hermetic, one that screens off from our view the intrinsic nature of what presents itself to us relationally in the guise of appearances. Since our inevitable ignorance of what lies behind that veil has no implications for the extent of our cognitive mastery of what we rightly call 'the real world', no concession is made to the scepticism of the previous generations in acknowledging this limit to proper cognitive ambition.

It was a further achievement of Kant's system to have shown how the world that is immediately presented to us by the senses must be a world of things that are independent of us, persisting when not perceived, and through and through united within a single absolute framework of space and time. There is necessity here at each of these points, and we need to be careful how it is expressed. The Kantian vision is that for any conscious subject, a world open to experience has to be so united, and has to be so just because there is no other material possibility for beings with our sort of mental endowment. Just because the idea of a world can only be introduced on the basis of experience that such subjects spontaneously fashion out of what is receptively and passively given, the phrase 'for any conscious subject' is effectively pleonastic. Understanding of the transcendental necessity that is involved cannot abstract from that.

It is the very same necessity that permits Kant to introduce causality into the world, namely, as what is required if we are to make objective judgements of simultaneity and succession. More than that, though, we have an explanation with a very modern ring to it of just how that idea with all its internal necessity is introduced into the empirical world, from which Hume had taught it to be inevitably absent. Our spontaneity in ordering the manifold gives us the power to ensure that there is strict universality in causal generalizations just because it is up to us to refuse to allow the world to present us with counter-examples to particularly marked regularities. Such regularities are 'materially necessary' (A227/ B279) and *a priori* in that their modality results from ourselves and from our being obliged to synthesize experience categorially in ways such as these if we are to enjoy objective experience of a world at all.

Hume's reductive conception of causality had made it impossible for him to appeal to anything other than psychologically rooted association when looking for justification of our inductive practices. Kant is in a far stronger position. The understanding's *a priori* need to synthesize a world in accordance with strict laws provides a guarantee of induction's reliability. That does not, of course, guarantee the propriety of just any inductive practice whatever, but then no one in their right mind should want that. What it is sensible to look for is some explanation why we must judge the future to be like the past (in some respects), and some guidance about which inductive practices are defensible, some guidance about those respects in which it is reasonable to expect the future to be like the past.

The first of these two demands Kant has already met in his response to Hume on the necessity of causation. As for the second, we should trust particular patterns of inductive reasoning to the extent that we find their conclusions incorporated in the account of the world we come to fashion under the Principles of the Understanding and the guidance of Reason as it directs us to synthesize the manifold of sense in ways which 'give these concepts the greatest possible unity combined with the greatest possible extension' (A644/B672). Of course, we make mistakes about which spontaneous ways of thinking, which attempts at employment of the imagination, approach or achieve maximal system, but that does nothing to inhibit our saying that a particular inductive practice is one it is reasonable to follow as long as we believe it draws on what we take to be the best systematic account we can give of the world at a certain time, or contributes to making our view of the world at that time maximally systematic. Once we see that the account of the world to which it makes its contribution is bettered by another, either on account of enjoying greater unity or greater extent, then the inductive practice that supported the less unified or narrower view of the world is no longer rationally supported. That is Kant's implicit response to the second question.

One topic which earlier thinkers had not been able to integrate into their accounts of the physical world – and not just because their accounts of the physical world were themselves defective – was that of the self. Here, too, I have suggested that Kant's system shows the way forward, though he is not particularly insistent about it, and it may even be that he did not appreciate the strength of his own underlying position. Kant's predecessors all identified the self as the thinking subject, but none of them had a satisfactory account of the self's relation to the body. Kant's overall *a priori* methodology requires that the self have its position in time, and hence also in space, and it allows that what is sometimes given to inner sense is the subject's own body and its states. Since it is a requirement of understanding that any empirically given state has to be the state of some substance-in-appearance, it makes good sense to think that the empirical self is nothing other than the living body. Here what starts out as a speculative hypothesis in our way of thinking about ourselves should eventually, under the pressure of systematic integration of our understanding of the world, become a kind of truism. So, at the end of the day, we should find it quite natural to say that as we find ourselves enjoying perceptual experience of one kind or another that is the way our bodies are registering their surroundings to themselves. As I attribute this position to Kant, it is rather different from anything we would today express when we say that the self is the functioning body, because for Kant the body is the phenomenal appearance of some ultimately noumenal substance. Even so, when we reflect on the implications of Kant's variety of holism, the philosophical move that lies within his grasp at this point is truly revolutionary.

This swift recapitulation of some of the main rewards of Kant's Copernican thinking may make it sound strange to say that he saw further than others by standing on the shoulders of giants. He appears to have rejected so much that his predecessors taught that one might think it better to say that he saw more by standing on the same ground as they, only by turning his head in a more rewarding direction. That image is not helpful though, and only serves to obscure what we ought to recognize: that is, just how much Kant is indebted to his forerunners. In the first place, sound appreciation of their ideas was necessary for him to be able to pin down errors that they had made, and to avoid them. (That almost goes without saying.) More germane than this to the analogy with Newton, though, is to notice what it is that his predecessors had assumed and what Kant had taken over from them, either as it stood or with some measure of adjustment. A number of things spring immediately to mind.

However dismissive Kant is of Berkeley, and however anxious lest his own Empirical Realism be conflated with what he regards as Berkeley's empirical idealism, in three respects Kant is deeply indebted to the good bishop. It was Berkeley's merit to have shown, in the *Three Dialogues between Hylas and Philonous*, how hopeless it was to try and construct inferences from the ideas that Descartes and Locke (and, of course, Berkeley himself) thought to be immediately given to us in perception. Curiously enough, Kant spends no time in the *Critique* making out the point in any detail, and his reader will need to recall the force of Berkeley's arguments against Locke at this point to appreciate the full power of the Refutation of Idealism. As he does so, he should consider just what would be the correct articulation of the content of those primitive 'ideas' from which Kant's opponents (Berkeley included) proposed to set out. The paucity of inferential potential that they offer springs far more evidently to view once one recognizes the illegitimacy of thinking of them as its appearing to one as if such and such were the case. Inferences to such and such's actually being the case would for them have to start out from something much farther back than that. As soon as this is realized, those inferences reveal themselves as entirely speculative. For that reason among others, Berkeley thought it was a far better to appeal to God as the explanatory source of our experiential ideas than to any hypothesized material cause (*Principles of Human Knowledge*, §72).

A second point at which Kant is indebted Berkeley lies in recognizing that in experience the world must be given to us immediately, not so much represented as presented. In this Berkeley was quite right, only since he was wedded to the same starting point as Descartes and Locke, he had little option but to identify the contents of the world with his ideas, construed either categorically or hypothetically (*Principles of Human Knowledge*, §§1–3). In the *Critique*, we see Kant taking over this insight of Berkeley's, and struggling to detach it from the kind of idealism which, rather unjustly, he thought left no room for a proper distinction between reality and illusion.[1]

Thirdly, we saw in the last chapter how Kant's conception of the truth-directedness of judgement was coherence-oriented. That was notably so in the way in which objectivity was ultimately judged in terms of approximation to a transcendentally presupposed norm of maximal extensiveness and systematicity. Interestingly, it is precisely such a notion of system that Berkeley himself appealed to in defending himself against the objection that his own form of idealism had no place for a distinction between truth and illusion, as Kant was later to object. This parallel between their two positions at this point should encourage one to find a more fundamental source of disagreement between them. To my way of thinking, this can only lie in the recognition that was central to Kant, but which entirely eluded Berkeley, that the unavoidably spatio-temporal character of experience entails that it be experience of a material world. It is Berkeley's denial of that that makes his own claim to systematicity jejune, and Kant's accusation that he reduces all to illusion ultimately so telling.

Stepping back now a couple of generations, from Descartes Kant had absorbed the ambition to provide the philosophical underpinning for a rigorously scientific and largely mechanistic account of the world.[2] Descartes' own revolution in philosophy may have misfired, but the overall aim that he had embraced was one that no one had brought any closer to realization since his day. Then too, strangely, the very sort of inference that Descartes had sought to rely on in taking us from the contents of the mind to the world beyond was to serve Kant well once he had readjusted the Cartesian starting point in the way we have seen in discussing the Refutation. At the end of the *Sixth Meditation*, Descartes tells us to use conjointly the faculties of mind given us by God, that is, to accept inferences comprehensively supported by sensation, memory and understanding (observation and theory) that would best explain the data to hand. Kant's own methodology for extending our cognitive reach beyond what is immediately given to us in perception is Cartesian enough at this point, and Kant would have had no reason to deny that.

On the reading of the *Critique* I have proposed, Kant's greatest debt to his predecessors is surely neither to Descartes nor to Berkeley, but to Locke. For at the heart of the motivation for Transcendental Idealism we find Kant struggling to make good deficiencies in Locke's account of concept-formation, which apart from its handling of concepts he found to be *a priori*, he took to be more or less acceptable. We can think of Kant as applying Locke's theory of Books II and III of the *Essay* with far greater rigour than Locke himself had done, and supplementing that story where it would not work not by appeal to the innateness of those ideas, but with a picture of fixed mental structure that secures the concepts *space*, *time* and the categories as framework concepts of an entirely non-empirical kind.

In this way Kant is able to treat the manifold of intuition – which is, at base, nothing other than the array of sensations, impressions or perceptions that provided Locke and his followers with their simple ideas of sensation – as the source of elementary empirical concepts which, together with those *a priori* concepts, we draw on to fashion our experience and knowledge of the surrounding world. It would of course be quite wrong to say that Kant was merely improving on the empiricist programme of the *Essay*, if only because he had little interest in developing a systematic account of concept-formation. Nevertheless, the whole thrust of the Copernican revolution that he offers stems from his attempt to put right something that he took Locke to have got badly wrong. Had he been less Lockean about what he took to be the genuinely empirical concepts that that left over, his philosophy would have had a very different character indeed.

In these various ways, then, Kant appropriated much from his predecessors as well as rejecting much, and what he appropriated drove him in the direction of the Copernicanism of which he was so proud. Yet however much we may admire his achievement at the end of the eighteenth century, his own teaching does not have many adherents today. Few find much that is compelling in Transcendental Idealism, nor in the kind of empirical realism that Kant thought was then left open to us. So, by way of closing, it is reasonable to ask what it is that has turned us away from the revolution that Kant had sought to institute, and more briefly, why reluctance to follow him does not simply reintroduce the kinds of impasse from which he thought he could release us.

Both in the Aesthetic and in the Analytic Kant's thought is governed by the conviction that the basic concepts we employ in the formulation of our experience are ineliminably non-empirical, and hence *a priori*. In according them this status we take them to be deeply lodged as guiding forms within the structure of the mind itself. Anyone who seeks to query this approach to Kant's Copernicanism can probe his development of the fulcral point in respect either of sensibility or of understanding. Should this probing be successful along either pathway, a route would then be open to treating Kant's allegedly 'formal' concepts as straightforwardly empirical. They would be seen as belonging to what he called the 'matter' of experience, not its form. In consequence, any knowledge we might acquire through their deployment could reasonably be taken to be knowledge of the world in itself and not merely of the world as it presents itself to us in idiosyncratically fashioned appearance. Then Kant would indeed still have initiated a revolution is philosophy – experience would yield direct and unmediated knowledge of the world, and much of it in fundamentally propositional form – but, despite his clamour to the contrary, the experiential knowledge that we normally and unquestioningly take ourselves to have of the in-itself would be just that, knowledge of the in-itself. The philosophical heavens would still revolve around their traditional fixed point, and no far-reaching Copernican adjustment of the going way of ordering them would then be called for.

Take the issue from the side of understanding. It is remarkable that Kant is almost completely silent about what makes a concept an empirical one. In the Metaphysical Deduction, he has very little to say explicitly about the *a priori* nature of the categories, introducing it as what is needed to unify the various empirical elements of our experience in judgement that are apt to express it. The underlying thought here is, I believe, the Lockean one that the empirical elements of a judgement can be identified in terms of sensorily given items (ultimately, the 'simple ideas' of the *Essay*) and that what does not find its place there must be *a priori* because otherwise we shall be committed to an unending regress. Allowing the categorial ideas to be empirical would give rise to a call for further elements to unite the larger panoply of empirical elements in the form of judgement assessable for objectivity, and then they too would have to be non-empirical and *a priori*, unless in their turn...and so on.

If the turn to Copernicanism depends on the identification of particular concepts as *a priori*, then the approach to that position from the side of the understanding can be blocked once one abandons the Lockean assumption that I presume Kant to be taking more or less for granted. Rather than delimiting the empirical by isolating individual sensory elements in experience, one might, curiously enough, do better to set out from a more truly Kantian understanding of experience, and say that any concept that identifies a compositional element of that will count as empirical. So, to take a single example, if my experience is of some men and women planting an avenue of trees, we need not say just that the concepts *men, women, planting* and *trees* are empirical ones (supposedly complex ideas built out of Lockean simples, as it were), but also the 'formal' concepts *and* and *some* have good claim to be empirical too since what my experience has presented me with is just that: some men and women planting trees. Furthermore, looking at it in this way, and taking the whole proposition as basic rather than its individual (Lockean) elements, we need not be embarrassed by the thought that still other (and so necessarily *a priori*) concepts must be supplied to unify the ones now taken to be empirical. The reason is that the propositional starting point already has its unity. That is not something that still needs to be provided, and provided from within the mind itself.

The non-empirical *a priori* character of a given concept, then, was determined for Kant by its unamenability to the established picture of concept-formation as set out in Locke's *Essay*, canonically at II.i and III.iii–vi. Its resistance to that model would be evidenced in either of two ways. Empirical abstraction of a concept would be impossible, first, if, when rigorously handled, experience itself shows up nothing to which the concept could be applied. Then there would simply be no available basis in experience from which the putative abstractive process could set out. We are, of course, supposing that we are dealing here with irreducible concepts, and not constructible complex ones like *phlogiston* or *unicorn* or maybe even *God*; but in the case of *space*, *time* and the categories this would be a reasonable enough thing to think, and Kant would certainly not contest it. The other obstacle to an abstractive account of a concept's acquisition is that any experiential base from which we might endeavour to abstract it should already have to be thought of in terms of the very concept whose acquisition we are looking to account for.

In the case of the categories, Kant is drawn to the first sort of justification of their apriority. Very much under the influence of Hume, he takes it that neither distinct and independent existence of bodies (substances) nor a cause's power to necessitate its effect are directly present in the matter of intuition. They have to be imported from the side of the mind itself. So at A112 he writes: 'All attempts to derive these pure concepts of the understanding from experience, and so to ascribe to them a merely empirical origin are entirely useless and vain. I need not insist upon the fact that, for instance, the concept cause involves the character of necessity, which no experience can yield'. In the case of the concepts *space, time* and their various derivatives, we have already seen how Kant believes that they fall to the second obstacle. 'Space is not an empirical concept which has been derived from outer experiences. For in order that certain sensations be referred to something outside me...the representation of space must be presupposed' (A23/B38). 'Time is not an empirical concept that has been derived from experience. For neither coexistence nor succession would ever come within our perception, if the representation of time were not presupposed as underlying them *a priori*' (A30/B46).

About the first of these lines of thought, it is ironic that it is in large part due to Kant himself that it came to be appreciated how inadequate was the very narrow conception of experience that animated empiricist thinking. A crucially important aspect of Kant's revolution was precisely the recognition that we have immediate sensory experience of substances standing in causal relations to one another. We see the hounds kill the fox; we surprise the vandals graffitoing the bus, and so on. In the light of this one might well think that the concepts in question are perfectly good candidates for empirical acquisition along the lines I sketched a couple of paragraphs back. There remains the special case of causation. On that subject, and as an immediate temporary stopgap for now, it is in order to observe that whatever Kant says at A112, the necessity the categories generally involve is not one that is internal to those concepts themselves. There is nothing like that in the notion of *substance*, for instance; rather, it is simply that they are necessary for objective experience, as argued in the Transcendental Deduction, and that is not something that has any claim to be criterial of their *a priori* status.

What remains at issue must be whether the second obstacle to their being empirical concepts is conclusive. If we think of substantiality and causality and the other categorial concepts on Kant's list as open to experience, will any hope of acquiring them empirically stumble over our having to suppose we already possess them? If the answer is 'No', there will be no obvious motivation left for treating them as *a priori* in the way Kant thought we must.[3]

To make progress we do not in fact need to contest that any purely abstractive acquisition of the categorial concepts could not avoid presupposing them. That, after all, is quite plausible in the case of some categories like *reality* and *existence*, even if we might find it questionable for others. And, anyway, in the earlier discussion of the Aesthetic I did not seriously question it for the concepts *space* and *time*. Pursuit of the issue can simply be undercut by declining to accept the alternatives that Kant offers us in supposing that either concepts are empirically acquired by abstraction or else they are *a priori* and supplied from within the mind's own constitution. The assumption that a concept must be an integral part of our mental make-up if it cannot be abstracted from experience in the approved manner does not resist scrutiny.

Very often we find that we enrich our conceptual stock by inventing ways to think about the world that might help us to explain or understand it, and we then go on to discover whether or not the world conforms to our new, hypothetical way of thinking. This is a procedure that is familiar and uncontroversial at the higher levels of theoretical enquiry, most notably in the natural sciences. And it shows that Kant's assumed model of concept acquisition is deeply at fault, just because, directed at such cases, it would force us either to deny that high-level theoretical concepts can be used to describe the world accurately, or else to accept that to the extent they do have application, they must either be reducible to more basic observational ones or else be *a priori* contributions to the world supplied by our own minds. For the concepts in point neither alternative is remotely plausible, and Kant's own appeal to the importance of theoretical concepts in the physical sciences plainly suggests that he will welcome an alternative route to the acquisition of notions he would certainly count as empirical and not *a priori*.

Given that the dichotomy of concepts into empirically abstractable or else *a priori* fails at the higher level, there is every reason to suppose that it fails at the more primitive levels too. It is eminently reasonable to suppose that from a very early age human beings, through a process of naive speculation, trial and error, and in progression first to simple conceptualization and then to more developed ways of thought, come to stock their minds with notions that answer to the complexities of the world that confronts them. The very thing we are familiar with at the higher reaches of investigative and theoretical thought is properly seen as a development of something available to us from the very start in more elementary form. Just because Kant is bound to appeal to the power of the imagination in fashioning the empirical concepts he needs for the expression of theoretical complexity in the natural sciences – concepts like *magnetism*, or *comet*, say – he could be expected to have some sympathy with the invitation to see the same kind of process working much more extensively in the construction of our more elementary conceptual stock.

In the case of the concepts *space* and *time*, we may indeed have to begin by locating something at a place and at a time, but these ideas can be ones we are all disposed to come to by being constantly confronted at times with things located at places, and discovering that to think of them as being so located enables us to make sense of the experience that we have. In such a case, the relevant concepts are emphatically not acquired by abstraction. Neither do we need to say we have them by drawing on some natively fixed 'pure intuition'. Rather, they seem to be formed exploratively to answer to what confronts us, and are subsequently tested, refined and developed against the progressively more finely articulated experience that their initial rudimentary acquisition gradually enables us to come by. If this suggestion is correct – a suggestion ultimately to be confirmed or not by developmental psychology rather than philosophy – it is open to Kant's critic to say that in regard to the formal concepts of intuition and understanding, the concept-forming process is a progressive and entirely empirical one, though not one that we should suppose to be carried out in the manner traditionally assumed.

A few paragraphs back I left the categorial concept *causation* rather in the air. It calls for a comment of its own. Kant insists with some plausibility on the putatively non-empirical element of necessity in that concept, and in the course of discussion earlier on we saw that for him that was entirely attributable to the way in which we treat interesting generalizations as strictly universal – 'in such manner that no exception is allowed as possible' (B4). So the necessity he is alluding to is not really some mysterious *a priori* element of the concept; it is rather a matter of how we handle what is empirically given for the sake of organizational pay-off. Now, of course Kant will say, he *does* say, that the strict universality that results is not derived from experience and that it is valid absolutely *a priori* (ibid.), but to this his critic can surely reply that in order to come by the concept of strict universality in non-*a priori fashion* we are not obliged to recognize any particular underlying generalization as strict. All that is necessary is that we hypothesize strictness in making sense of our experience. That does not entail that it is only realized by some kind of decision of ours, as Kant appears to suggest, since, after all, whether there are unfailing generalizations can perfectly well depend on what the world is like independently of how we allow ourselves to think about it. The appeal of Kant's own idea here simply rides on the back of the thought that unless strictness were immediately open to view we should have to account for our possession of the idea in non-empirical terms. Once that assumption is abandoned, the original claim of the concept *cause* to be necessity-involving and as such demanding special treatment loses its appeal. To say this naturally leaves the issue of the centrality of the role of that concept in our understanding of the world, its necessity for objective experience, undisturbed. That is just as it should be.

In the expository material of chapters 3 and 4 I have emphasized the importance to Kant of the notions of *objective validity*, of *the affinity of the manifold* and of the *necessary conformity of nature to law*. For him these are all necessary concepts in that self-conscious experience would be impossible unless permeated by them, and moreover they are *a priori* ones too because in his programme they are the manifestation in our experience of the *a priori* categorial concepts that our various forms of judgement bring with them. Since we now have a way of resisting the thought that these latter concepts are *a priori*, that resistance will naturally carry over to these higher-order concepts that are dependent on them. The effect of this will be to leave the Copernican aspect of Kant's revolution without compelling motivation at its deepest point since that stems entirely from accepting the *a priori* character of these so-called formal' ideas. It will also encourage us to ask not just whether the conception of experience we are left with is as narrow as Descartes, Locke, Berkeley and Hume took it to be, but whether the very much broader conception of it that Kant encouraged us to adopt in Copernican vein should not be embraced independently of his turn towards mind-constituted 'appearances', as experience *tout court*, that is. To take that step would be to think of Kant's 'formal' concepts as empirical ones, only 'empirical' in a larger sense than it has in his own vocabulary.

The upshot is that while Kant did indeed find a novel way of dealing with the epistemological worries of the previous century, in the absence of other arguments strong enough to force us along his own aprioristic path, there is no reason to pay the price he urges us to part with. Saving that caveat, we shall say that we do indeed immediately experience the world of causally interrelated substances immovably situated in space and time. That is the true extent of Kant's revolution. However, the experienced world is the absolute, real, world, and not the world of Kantian appearance. It would be quite misleading, tendentious even, for Kant to suppose that the world's reality is here being inappropriately treated as 'transcendent' or 'transcendental' as he might well be inclined to do. This is just because treating his 'formal' concepts as empirical leaves us with nothing to transcend.

The last point deserves to be stated in a way that confronts it with Kant's own manner of expressing himself. In the General Observations on Transcendental Aesthetic, by way of confirmation of the ideality of all objects of the senses, Kant insists that everything we are aware of in sense is either a qualification of extension or motion or moving forces, and that all of these are to be understood as relations (implicitly relations to ourselves in one way or another). 'What it is that is present at this or that location, or what it is that is operative in the things themselves apart from change in location is not given in intuition. Now a thing in itself cannot be known through mere relations; and we may therefore conclude that since outer sense gives us nothing but mere relations, this sense can contain in its representation only the relation of an object to the subject, and not the inner properties of the object in itself' (B67). In this passage Kant clearly takes the primary qualities of objects (extension, location, motion) as what we would see as secondary – accounted for in relation to us – and his reason for this is because of the *a priori* and non-empirical nature of the concepts *space* and *time*. Once we find a way to treat them as fully empirical, none of the triad extension, motion and moving forces will be explained in terms of 'relation of an object to the subject'. Consequently, we shall be in just the position we want to be in if our experience of the world is to be experience of it as it is in itself, and, unlike Kant, we shall then be able to bring within our cognitive grasp 'the inner properties of the object in itself'. Behind these objects lie no others, and since it is these to which experience gives us access, the realism that is here expressed cannot be called 'transcendental'. It is empirical realism but not Empirical Realism; Empirical Realism, that is, without appearances.

These observations are not intended as a refutation Kant's overall Copernican position. They do, however, deprive it of a great deal of the motivation that persuaded him to adopt it, and without which it lacks the sort of intellectual support he believed it had. That is a serious enough flaw, but a more fundamental difficulty comes with the way in which Kant struggled to free himself from the legacy of his predecessors. This comes out in a striking way when we consider an apparently inevitable mismatch between the notion of objectivity that he makes central to his metaphysic of experience and the content accruing to that notion which his metaphysic is actually able to hold in place. If the mismatch is correctly identified its effect will be to undermine from within the realism that Kant recommends us to adopt. The reader will decide whether the threat here outlined can be satisfactorily countered within the framework that Kant thinks himself entitled to draw on.

Consider the inner lives of two people separated by a span of some centuries. The manifold of intuition that is theirs is synthesized in time, and, as the last sentence intimates, that time is one that encompasses the experience of both parties. That is a reflection of what we standardly, and with us, Kant, assume the transcendentally necessary time order to bring with it. How, though, is Kant to secure that interpersonal community for the mind's own form of inner sense? It can only be from the way in which we find our representations brought within the framework of time, which Kant points out is infinite, unified and unique. Yet, the way in which that infinity, unity and uniqueness are manifest to each one of us is only by commanding the experience of the individual subjects that we are. Thus, as regards the unity of time, I know that any experience

I might have must find its place in the same time order as any other experience I might have. I know that time is infinite or unlimited in that no matter how many more episodes my inner life might contain there will always be a moment in time to which they can be assigned. What is entirely lacking in this thought is any indication of how my temporal experience can be located in the same temporal frame as yours, or how the experience of our two imagined subjects may be separated by so many centuries. I may of course on occasion have an experience *as* of you giving expression to your inner life, but that will be an episode of *my* inner life, not of yours. So it would seem that the form of intuition that is given to us as a matter of pure intuition and whose fundamental character is revealed in the way each of us is obliged to order the manifold of our experience not only does not, but, more importantly, *could not* embrace the communal aspect that we regularly take it to have.

How could Kant have passed over this pressing question? And is the issue one that he can remedy? The first of these queries is easier to answer than the second. In the absence of any developed predicate logic, an illegitimate slide from 'We are obliged to order our experiences within a unified time-frame' to 'There is a unified time-frame within which we are obliged to unify our experiences' may simply have passed Kant by. The first does allow for each of us to order our experience in unified time-frames proper only to ourselves, enjoying no community, whereas the second does not. In characterizing the form of inner sense, Kant gives us reason to insist upon the first, but it is the second that he needs to secure.

The oversight is perhaps further encouraged by the way in which Kant finds it entirely natural, and entirely in line with the kind of communitarian constructivism we found him adopting in his approach to objectivity and truth, to speak of the mind [*das Gemüt*] in generic terms, and very rarely in terms of the intuitional contents available to the individual thinker. So, to take a typical example, at A33/B50 he writes: 'Since all representations, whether they have for their objects outer things or not, belong, in themselves, as *determinations of the mind, to our inner state* [*als Bestimmungen des Gemüts, zum innern Zustande gehören*]; and since *this inner state* [*dieser innere Zustand*] stands under the formal conditions of inner intuition, and so belongs to time, time is an *a priori* condition of all appearance whatsoever' (emphases added). Given the way in which the mind is spoken of in these passages and their like quite generally, it is very natural to suppose that the unity of time must be the unity of the same time for the generic subject, that is for any subject, for the sensibility-dependent or, simply, the human mind. In reality, though, this is at best an unsupported assumption and if it is to be made good, the generic idea will need to be introduced on the basis of a story the concerns individual members of the genus. It must be from their individual experience that the interpersonal structure of the form of intuition is discerned. Proceeding as Kant proceeds just leaves this desired community unaccounted for.

To work round the difficulty Kant cannot appeal to temporal relations holding between things in themselves, since in his book the very idea is a nonsense (A34–5/B51, B70). Nor can he simply appeal to our everyday concept of time, since that has to be controlled for legitimacy from within the resources of the Metaphysical Exposition, which is too weak for the task. The only resource open to him would seem to be to draw on his anti-Cartesian insight of the Refutation of Idealism to the effect that inner experience is only possible through outer experience (B277), and hence through our immediate awareness of outer objects, distinct from ourselves, but in principle common to all. Such objects (appearances, of course, not things in themselves) we have to think of as having determinate temporal duration even in the absence of our experience of them, so we might suppose that that fact about them will be exploitable as opening up the structure of a shared temporal form of intuition as our common way of thinking requires.

But is it? In the first place, the idea of my time extending to moments when I am experiencing nothing, and so not aware of the external world – in sleep, say, or under anaesthetic – is easily enough handled within the limits of Kant's own Metaphysical Exposition by the reflection that my unified time extends to all moments at which I *might* have experience, and hence to moments at which I am as it just happens unaware of the external world I experience in my conscious waking life. So, the time-frame within which my external objects persist cannot yet be said to extend any further than that.

Secondly, the spatial form of outer intuition which is being invoked here to save the situation suffers from a completely analogous difficulty of its own. Space is a unified whole; I cannot but synthesize all outer experience within one infinite and unified space. But that says no more than that there is one unified space for *my* manifold of intuition; it does not say that all our various manifolds, yours and mine and the Queen of Sheba's, are synthesized or are synthesizable as belonging to one common space. The reasons are the same as before, so the thought that we might appeal to a common outer intuition to secure what inner intuition fails to provide is entirely question-begging. What is common to us all is the structure of both inner and outer intuition; but that structure is not of an inner or an outer intuition that is common.

As a last resort one might considering relaxing Kant's thought that the forms of inner and outer sense be conceived of as particulars, and saying instead that intuition has to be ordered spatially and temporally, where such *a priori* ordering brings with it uniqueness and infinity and continuity in the way that Kant takes to be essential. If in this way we move to a generalized and relational conception of space and time, the question of whether my particular time could be the same as yours may appear to be by-passed since we both order things in the very same way. True, the question as posed recedes; but it has not completely disappeared because it now becomes important to ask whether the objects and events that are the experiential output of the mind's (or, better, minds') synthetic activity, with its manifold intuitional flow as input, can be identified across different experiencing subjects. Only if they can shall we be able to make the sort of judgement that this discussion started out from, the judgement, for example, that my great-grandfather's earliest experience of his surroundings occurred about two hundred years before my experience of typing these lines.

What this comes to is at the very least the pressing need to identify places and times across different subjects' experience, and as before the difficulty is to know how that is to be done when we set out along the path of synthetic construction from manifolds private to the individuals whose manifolds they are. That they should be systematically congruous with one another—as if that were an independently knowable matter! – would not settle the issue.[4] Once that is acknowledged, it is hard to see what else might turn the trick other than some forbidden foray into the causal powers of the same elements of the in-itself to produce congruent manifolds in different subjects' experience. At this point it is a challenge to the sympathetic reader to find a way forward that might be congenial to Kant himself.

The importance of meeting the challenge is evident once the threat to the Kantian notion of objectivity is made clear. The categories, we saw, were at heart best thought of as individual manifestations of the normative nature of judgements that are embodied in a subject's experience of the world. The idea of objectivity that they expressed was essentially that anyone should concur with a given subject's categorially warranted judgements on pain of being mistaken. Now, when we reflect that the categories can only be brought to bear on what is provided by intuition, and intuition can only be intuition of things located in a spatio-temporal framework that threatens to be private to the individual subject, that normative core to the idea of objectivity can have no application. Whether a particular experiential judgement of mine is one that others should assent to or not is a question that cannot arise just because the location of its objects within forms of intuition accessible to me is precisely something from which others will be sealed off. No matter how closely others' experience may parallel my own, it cannot amount to experience of the very same things in their world of appearance as are given to me in mine. Consequently, there is no way in which the judgements others come to make could be rightly said to accord with mine, or even to fail to do so. The idea of communal objectivity thus collapses. With its fall, Kant's conception of nature as the set of all appearances necessarily unified in conformity to law also collapses. Even if it is an established necessity that our experience should conform to law, that the prevailing laws should be the same for each subject of experience is an entirely open matter, and the *a priori* unity of nature is thereby lost.

Kant would of course be quite horrified by this, and rightly so, for what he most prizes has now been turned head over heels. His way of ensuring that we have knowledge of the world around us through experience presenting us directly with the familiar shared spatio-temporal world of appearance now threatens to become the impossibility of there existing any such common world at all. It cannot be the world of things in themselves, since they are not in space and time; nor, it now emerges, can it be a 'real' world of appearance, since there is no possibility of our making objectively valid judgements of experience about that. Instead of being our saviour from the inherited mire of scepticism (guided by the peculiar motor of concept-formation that underlies his Copernicanism), Kant risks unwittingly becoming scepticism's ultimate advocate.

Is there any remedy to this looming danger? Not within Kant's own version of empirical realism, to be sure; none the less, there is scope enough for us to counter sceptical threats within empirical realism of another stripe. This is an empirical realism that acknowledges us to have much experiential knowledge of things in themselves, or better, of things *tout court*. Those things we must say are situated in a space and a time to which we all have access, but whose nature is in no way answerable to the structure of our sensibility-dependent minds. It must be a space and time that is of the world itself and as it is in itself.

Of course, Kant thinks there are insurmountable obstacles to any such way of thinking. First, we know that he would say we cannot account for our possession of the conceptual stock we would need to have to articulate such experience; and, then secondly, we should be unable to account for the synthetic *a priori* status of such truths as those recording the unified and infinite extent of the spatio-temporal world that this would-be 'transcendent' version of empirical realism envisages. For the restricted purpose of this discussion, it should be enough to indicate how his opposition might be overcome.

As for the first matter, we have already seen that Kant's account of concept-formation was unduly rigid. On that score nothing more need be said, except perhaps to emphasize how he had underplayed the importance of our natural capacity to think imaginatively and so to explore the world with an eye to furthering explanation and understanding of what it throws up. That maybe is the mind's true structure, only unlike in Kant's conception of it, this more modest conception of its working does not involve ascribing any particular content to the mind as part of its fundamental constitution. That Kant himself freely and repeatedly draws on the imaginative power of the mind in working out his communitarian synthesis of the manifold that results in scientific knowledge of the world suggests that this is a route he should be willing to explore.

The other, so far undiscussed, matter concerns the necessities of space and time themselves, not the allegedly *a priori* and non-empirical nature of the concepts *space* and *time*. Kant's thought was that if, *per impossibile*, it were a truth that the space and time of the in-itself were a unified space-time, then that could only be a contingent matter of fact. All substantive necessity would be lost, and that would be the ultimate, utterly unacceptable, absurdity. Now, unless we are verificationists and then go on to treat such claims as simply analytic, we may have to say that their absolute necessity is indeed an open question. But in an interesting way that concession can be seen to harmonize well enough with Kant's own style of thought. What we often take for an absolute, metaphysical, necessity is in fact a necessity that captures the limits of the knowledge we can have of the in-itself, not a necessity that concerns the in-itself itself. So, for example, were there to be, say, self-enclosed spaces or times, metaphysical black holes, as it were, they would inevitably lie beyond our cognitive grasp, and lie beyond it of necessity. For did our knowledge stretch that far, that itself would bring them within the unity of the space and time we do know. This, I say, is a perception that Kant himself should find congenial. For when he accounts for the unity of space and time, indeed when he accounts for the necessity of experience being spatio-temporal in kind, he does so by saying that that is the form of intuition which is ours and which we cannot envisage in any other way. That it is that way is not further explicable, a brute fact about the way our experience has to be (B145–6). But if he can say that about the substantive necessities of our forms of intuition, he is not at all well placed to object to analogous remarks being made about our understanding of the spatio-temporal nature of the in-itself, once we have overcome the first objection and earned our right to think about it in the first place.

At the outset I said that Kant supposed his combination of Transcendental Idealism and Empirical Realism to represent a neglected route to handling the epistemological problems inherited from earlier days. Not only that, but he also supposed it to be the only viable way of dealing with those issues. In the last pages I have suggested to the contrary that it was neither viable in its own right, nor did it exhaust the possibilities. A close contemporary of Kant's who saw this was Thomas Reid (1710–96), whose bluff advocacy of common sense in his *Inquiry into the Human Mind on the Principles of Common Sense* (1764) amounted to empirical realism without any restriction to the world of appearance, and hence amounted to what Kant was to ridicule as 'Transcendental Realism' (A369). In the light of his thoroughgoing attack on the Locke's 'way of ideas', Reid's work had acquired a notable following on the continent of Europe by the time Kant was writing the *Critique*. Curiously, it was work that Kant knew about and which, in his doctoral dissertation of 1770, he had dismissed as philosophically worthless. What needs to be understood is why that seemed to him so obviously the case.

To Kant it could not but appear that Reid's thinking was intellectually unsophisticated, and that it did no more than give expression to the prejudices of vulgar common sense without the support of philosophical discipline. In this, we see how Kant was still in lien to the view he fought so hard to overcome. Somehow the original ideational objects of acquaintance in the mind had to be retained, which is indeed what happens when experience is viewed as a synthesis of the manifold of intuition, and yet be combined with the idea that what is immediately given in experience is the external world itself. As Kant saw it, only his peculiar combination of Transcendental Idealism and Empirical Realism could hope to achieve that. His views about the constraints on concept-formation and the synthetic *a priori* nature of the fundamental truths about our experience convinced him that that combination enjoyed impregnable support. Seen from that stance, Reid's cavalier manner of by-passing the world of appearance altogether could only seem ridiculously naive. Yet once Kant's leading assumptions are shed, Reid's position takes on an entirely different mien. It will be dismissed only by those who remain caught within the orbit of those Cartesian ideas from which Kant had, in the end unsuccessfully, striven to free himself.

A Caveat by way of Afterword

Anyone who contemplates writing about Kant does well to reflect on the fifth of Thomas De Quincey's *Letters to a Young Man whose Education has been Neglected* [1823] (On the English Notices of Kant). Likewise, anyone who contemplates reading such an offering does well to do so with De Quincey's remarks before their mind.

The persons who originally introduced the Kantian philosophy to the notice of the English public, or rather attempted to do so, were two Germans – Dr Willich and (not long after) Dr Nitsch. Dr Willich, I think, has been gone to Hades for these last dozen years; certainly his works have: and Dr Nitsch, though not gone to Hades, is gone (I understand) to Germany, – which answers my purpose as well; for it is not likely that a few words uttered in London will contrive to find a man buried in the throng of thirty millions Germans. *Quoad hoc*, therefore Dr Nitsch may be considered no less defunct than Dr. Willich; and I can run no risk of wounding anybody's feelings if I should pronounce both doctors very eminent blockheads. It is difficult to say which wrote the more absurd book. Willich's is a mere piece of book-making, and deserves no sort of attention. But Nitsch, who seems to have been a painstaking man, has produced a work which is thus far worthy of attention, that it reflects as in a mirror one feature common to most of the German commentaries upon Kant's works, and which it is right to expose. With very few exceptions, these works are constructed upon one simple principle. Finding it impossible to obtain any glimpse of Kant's meaning or drift, the writers naturally asked themselves what was to be done. Because a man does not understand one iota of his author, is he therefore not to comment upon him? That were hard indeed, and a sort of abstinence which it is more easy to recommend than to practise. Commentaries must be written; and, if not by those who understand the system (which would be the best plan), then (which is clearly the second-best plan) by those who do *not* understand it. Dr Nitsch belonged to this latter very respectable body, for whose great numerical superiority to their rivals I can take upon myself to vouch. Being of their body, the worthy doctor adopted their expedient, which is simply this: never to deliver any doctrine except in the master's words; on all occasions to parrot the *ipsissima verba* of Kant; and not even to venture upon the experiment of a new illustration drawn from their own funds.

Notes

Chapter 1: Historical Prelude

1 At *Essay* IV.x.1, Locke does say of God's existence that 'this is the most obvious truth that reason discovers, and . . . its evidence (if I mistake not) equal to mathematical certainty'. In fact his reasoning is a standard cosmological proof: 'if we know there is some real being, it is an evident demonstration that from eternity there has been something' (IV.x.3), where the antecedent itself is not something that Locke can be allowed to take for granted. Hence the caveat 'in all consistency'. Kant's dismissive handling of the cosmological proof runs from A603/B631 to A614/B642.

2 Here and below page references are given, where useful, to the first edition of the *Critique* in the form A123, and to the second edition in the form B123. Where the text is common to the editions, pages are cited in both versions. Throughout I have used the English translation by N. Kemp Smith (Macmillan, 1929).

3 His way of making this point, so crucial to the history of the subject, is to say, in the *Second Meditation*: 'For although I am thinking about these matters within myself, silently and without speaking, nonetheless the actual words bring me up short, and I am almost tricked by ordinary ways of talking. We say that we see the wax itself, if it is there before us, not that we judge it to be there from its colour or shape; and this might lead me to conclude without more ado that knowledge of the wax comes from what the eye sees, and not from scrutiny of the mind alone. But then if I look out of the window and see men crossing the square, as I just happen to have done, I normally say that I see the men themselves, just as I say that I see the wax. Yet do I see any more than hats and coats which could conceal automatons? I *judge that* they are men. And so something which I thought I was seeing with my eyes is in fact grasped solely by the faculty of judgement which is in my mind' (*The Philosophical Writings of Descartes*, eds Cottingham, Stoothoff and Murdoch, vol. II (Cambridge: Cambridge University Press), p. 21).

4 The innately given concept to the fore in the Meditations is of course that of God, but Descartes' 1647 *Comments on a Certain Broadsheet* (Cottingham et al., vol. I, p. 304, 'In article *thirteen* . . . ') is explicit about many more, and an interesting rejection of the kind of empiricism that Locke was to develop so influentially in his *Essay* at the end of the century.

5 I stress, the manifold is not, for Kant, what we perceive. We make sense of that as we apply our minds to it interpretatively, finding thereby a way of experiencing the world in one way or another, as this or that. What we perceive is the world as it impinges on us and as it lends itself to be construed in one way or another.

6 It helps greatly to keep firmly in mind that Kant's use of 'appearance' is tied to his preoccupation with our lived experience of the world and that considerations about non-experiential knowledge strike him as being of secondary importance. There is something of this usage present today in the way a crusty schoolmaster might greet the arrival of a tardy pupil: 'Let us all pause to welcome Jones's appearance.' What is to be welcomed is not the class's perceptual input, nor the way they make sense of it, but the presence in their experience of their comrade Jones, his (belated) appearance.

7 Cf. A29, where Kant speaks of 'all kinds and determinations of space' (and of course time) as having to be represented *a priori*, if concepts of figures and of their relations are to arise.

8 Later on, we shall meet a further alternative also canvassed at the time, but one which did not seriously engage Kant and which he even regarded with a measure of contempt.

Chapter 2: Sensibility, Space and Time

1 'I entitle *transcendental* all knowledge which is occupied not so much with objects as with the mode of our knowledge of objects in so far as this mode of knowledge is to be possible *a priori*' (A11/B25). Somewhat confusingly, Kant also frequently uses the term 'transcendental' in a quite different sense to speak of what lies beyond appearance. So, by 'transcendental idealism' he means our inability to have any experience beyond what is provided to us in appearance (A28/B44, A36/B52, A296/B352, A369).

2 Indebtedness in these matters to 'the celebrated Locke' is expressed at A86/B118–19, where Kant insists that *a priori* concepts are not to be handled in the same way. There is no reason to think he is being ironic about Locke's achievement. He just sees it as less extensive than Locke himself took it to be.

3 Kant's word '*Vorstellung*', in English, 'representation', ranges over both perceptual images and conceptual thought and its elements, concepts. In this it is like Locke's 'ideas', and I shall disambiguate the usage without comment as and when it is helpful to do so.

4 Strictly speaking, the forms of intuition should govern intuitions directly only in the sense of 'sensations of the senses' (A177/B219) and not objects of experience. Then that the sensory flow is successive is answerable to the form of inner sense, time. How the world we experience is a temporally structured world is then accounted for (in the Analogies) by the way in which understanding synthesizes the manifold of intuition. But in outer sense the manifold of intuition (sensation) is taken to be enriched with representational content, in part both spatial and temporal, and it is very difficult for Kant to maintain a distinction between that (which at the outset is supposed not to draw on the work of understanding) and our representations of appearances (which does so draw). So the text of the Aesthetic happily speaks of the forms of intuition applying to objects of our sensible intuition. A footnote to B160 shows sensitivity to a greater complexity of the matter than is developed in the earlier pages.

5 However, in the context of a reflection about the original creation of the world at B251–2 he does make that point that when we think about things not as phenomena but as things in themselves, 'our terms would carry with them quite other meanings, and would not apply to appearances as possible objects of experience'.

6 If Transcendental Idealism is false in the sense that we do quite generally have knowledge of the world as it is in itself, then the empirical realism of Kant's brand will of course also be false.

7 They must have some such character, for if they didn't Kant would be unable to think of them as impressing themselves on our receptive sensibility.

8 A 'two-world' formulation of Kant's idealism is favoured in the A edition (notably at A249). In B, it generally yields to a better two-aspect conception of the matter.

9 In elaborating briefly his strategy for avoiding the contradiction at Bxxvii, Kant says he is taking the object (we might say here 'the world') 'in a twofold sense'. This is unfortunate, because as we view something from different points of view we don't pave the way for any ambiguity in the expressions designating what we come to talk about. The right thing for Kant to have said is that as we assess a proposition of the form 'x is F' for truth or falsehood, we need to make explicit whether the judgement in question is that x, taken in itself, is F or x, taken as it appears, is F. In both cases the sense of whatever term replaces 'x', as, for example, 'the world', will be one and the same.

10 Nor will it do for him to insist on the thought that secondary qualities can be different for different men, since that now only comes to the obvious truth that the same colour or taste can appear differently to different people. But since the comparison is between spatial properties and colour rather than the mere appearance of colour, the point falls.

11 See also A252 and A494/B523, both quoted in chapter 5 note 16 below.

12 At A109 we have: 'Appearances are the sole objects which can be given
    to us immediately, and that in them which relates immediately to the
    object is called intuition.' Although this sentence is taken from the
    Transcendental Deduction, it is clear that Kant thinks he is entitled to
    it from the discussion of the Aesthetic.

Chapter 3: Experience and Judgement

1 In a footnote to B160 Kant acknowledges that even the unity of space
   and time introduced in the Aesthetic at A25/B32 draws significantly on
   the operation of understanding. The thought must be that we can only
   come to experience a *unified* spatio-temporal world in the light of what
   goes on in the world, which itself depends on the extensive exercise of
   the understanding in ways to be discussed in chapter 5 below under the
   Analogies of Experience. So, to speak of the original *a priori* intuitions
   of Space and Time as providing a framework of experience does not by
   itself fix the character of that framework.
2 The 'have to' of this sentence is implicitly conditional, 'have to' *if* the
   deliverances of sense and understanding are to be brought together in
   the experience of any given individual, as they must if the individual is
   to have experience at all. Although I do not discuss it until the next
   chapter, the presence of the unity of apperception is already making
   itself felt here.
3 The whole section itself bears the title 'Transcendental Logic'. The
   Analytic is its main positive half, and the Dialectic the more polemically
   directed portion.
4 An exception is Spinoza, who deprecated the equation of thought and
   image at *Ethics*, II.49, Scholium. There is little evidence though that
   Kant knew his work well or had occupied himself with it in any detail.
5 The passage of the *Critique* I have been drawing on runs from A50/B74
   to A70/B95, straddling the general discussion of Logic and the first
   pages of the Analytic of Concepts.
6 The term 'metaphysical deduction' occurs at B159, not as a section
   heading, but descriptively to stress the *a priori* nature of the concepts in
   question. It can be seen as a reminder of the parallel between the
   discussion of sensibility and understanding.
7 '*Leitfaden*', alluding to the thread of Ariadne that enabled Theseus to
   escape from the labyrinth after slaying the Minotaur.

Chapter 4: Understanding, Objectivity and Self-consciousness

1 Readers of the Metaphysical Deduction anxious not to stray far from
   Kant's text might prefer to hear the expression 'introduce a transcendental content' of A79/B105 as indicating no more than that each form
   of judgement can be expected to make its impact on the content of the

experience to which it contributes. That would leave it an open question whether a distinct transcendental content would be in play with each form of judgement or whether the same content would be present each time, though articulated in a different guise. It would then fall to the Transcendental Deduction to settle that question in favour of the second alternative.

2 See also *Prolegomena* §19, which characterizes objective validity in terms of necessary and universal validity. In either case it would be important to note that what judgement does is to advance a thought as true; it does not itself guarantee its truth. So truth-aptness might be a better notion for Kant to use here than truth itself. Employment of the categories in judgement cannot block sceptical queries without further ado. Judgements and experience may necessarily aspire to truth, but whether they achieve it, and when, is a distinct issue.

3 To make this point should in no way obscure the importance Kant attributes to understanding's normative concern with truth. Not only are judgements put forward as true; in addition, they are accepted (they articulate the synthesis of the manifold we actually come to in experience) only as they appear to contribute to, or fit in with, the 'connected whole of human knowledge' that we build up over time. Briefly, whether or not the objectively valid experiential judgements we make are in fact true, they are always adopted in the light of a concern for truth. Judgement aims at knowledge, and understanding is the faculty of judgement (A69/B94). We may suppose that the propositions of speculative metaphysics that Kant criticizes in the Dialectic fail to be objectively valid, not because they fail of truth, but because they do not resist the close scrutiny of reason.

4 'Criterion' here is to be taken evidentially as a way of telling, in Kant's words, a 'general test of the truth of such content' (A59/B83). The stupidity of seeking any such absolutely general criterion is there likened to that of trying to catch the milk from a he-goat by holding a sieve beneath it, perhaps the only recognizable joke in the whole *Critique*.

5 In the case of a presumably objectively valid, yet none the less false judgement, necessarily anyone who makes the same judgement as I do, will be getting things wrong. (In the *Prolegomena*, Kant contrasts such cases with judgements that are merely subjectively valid, citing the case of one person's reports on his feeling as having no implication about what anyone else should say.)

6 At A251 Kant puts it by saying: 'Consequently it [the transcendental object, A.S.] is not in itself an object of knowledge, but only the representation of appearances under the concept of an object in general – a concept which is determinable through the manifold of these appearances.'

7 If it is preferred to the alternative I suggest it would emphasize Kant's repeated claim that experiential judgements have ultimately to answer

to something in the world independently of the way in which it appears, and that objective validity demands more than passing the test of understanding's critical scrutiny. The trouble is that this extends way beyond anything that the categories can ensure, which is the focus of this part of the discussion.

8 On the other hand, it could be argued that its presence here testifies to its non-redundancy, hence to the appeal of the 'noumenal' reading that I have declined. To adopt that reading would then align objective validity and truth more closely than I have done, and leave Kant's own assimilation of them at A125 in place. Its absence from the B edition Deduction would then call for explanation. (It does appear in its noumenal guise elsewhere in B, as for example at A494/B522.)

9 A term we find central to Leibniz's conception of the mental life of the kind humans enjoy. See for example *Monadology* §14: 'The passing state that contains and represents a multitude in the one, or in the simple substance, is what is called perception. This must be distinguished from apperception, or conscious awareness . . . '

10 At B148 Kant makes the contrast between the categories and the pure intuitions of Space and Time, saying that unlike the latter, the pure concepts of understanding 'extend to objects of intuition in general, be their intuition like or unlike ours, if only it be sensible and not intellectual'. The thought that it must be sensible in those other cases, must surely be about sensibilities unlike ours in not being spatio-temporal. At the end of the same paragraph Kant says 'Only *our sensible* and empirical intuition can give to them body and meaning', but that can only be the thought that it is only for us that *our* sort of sensible intuition can give the categories 'body and meaning'.

11 I put it like this so as to leave open the question whether our representing the world as law-governed in this or that way itself gives us knowledge of it. At various places Kant does explicitly say that experience is knowledge (e.g. B218), but that is not something that the Transcendental Deduction yet puts him in a position to assert any more than it entitles him to say that objective validity is truth.

12 This line of thought could be extended to Kant's treatment of the axioms of Euclidean geometry in the Aesthetic, shielding him from the conventional objection that other geometries show them not to be necessary.

Chapter 5: The Principles of Pure Understanding

1 Even though Kant accepted Newtonian universal gravitation and sought some metaphysical underpinning for it in the Third Analogy, he still endorsed a form of Cartesian mechanism, assuming that gravitational forces work not directly and at a distance but through the medium of the all-pervasive ether.

2 Curiously, the argument is not explicitly stated at A164–5/B204–5, where Kant discusses the topic of quantity. But B206 makes it plain that he thinks he has secured for arithmetic what the immediately preceding passage did for geometry.

3 In consistency with what was said in chapter 2, 'no more than' must be understood as itself an exaggeration. Strictly speaking, they could not possess magnitude of any sort, and hence not be thought of in mathematical terms at all. The last sentence of the Anticipations (A166/B207) makes the point explicitly.

4 Although it is of course not a metaphysical truth, in Kant's eyes the *a priori* principle embodied in the Anticipations lends colour to the thought that there can be no action at a distance and that universal gravitation must operate through the presence of ether evenly distributed throughout space.

5 'Dynamical' because providing the fundamental *a priori* truths governing questions of movement of matter through space and time, questions of mechanics, that is, or, more particularly, and abstracting from matter at rest, *dynamical* ones.

6 In the end, it may be more accurate to Kant's ultimate position to say that what is conserved is force rather than matter, since he has a view of matter as being constituted by attractive and repulsive forces, only this aspect of his philosophical dynamics is not much in evidence in the *Critique*, apart from a remark at A265/B321.

7 Leaning on the Anticipations of Perception, we might even view this as a world with fluctuating intensive magnitude. We should abstract here from the downright falsity of the conservation of absolute mass (mass being lost as converted into energy) just in order to get at Kant's own argument for the conservation principle.

8 'If, then, a judgment is thought with strict universality, that is, *in such a manner that no exception is allowed as possible* [my emphasis, A.S.], it is not derived from experience, but is valid absolutely *a priori*' (B4).

9 Also, of course, Kant thinks of conceptual necessities as analytic, and not even the basic Principles of Understanding are that.

10 In fact Kant even asserts that the parsimony of principles is not only an economical requirement of reason but is itself one of nature's own laws (A650/B678).

11 I am taking Kant's 'criterion' here as evidential for truth rather than constitutive of it, in line with his own classical usage. It cannot be constitutive since that would make global systematic error a logical impossibility, analytically so on Kant's understanding, and it is certainly not that. Also, it makes better sense to take Kant at his word as he proclaims a correspondence version of truth (of a sort), and not to replace that with a coherence story. The difficulty of course is to introduce the corresponding term, since that cannot simply be the synthesized appearances, which will be the same whether our experiential judgement

is true or not. I have tentatively suggested at various places that the desired term must be that in the world as it is in itself which affects us in the best of cases with the systematic appearances we arrive at, both actual and hypothetical. Here, again, reflection on the proper construction of Kant's 'transcendental object' could be recommended.

12 That point of maximal systematicity must lie within experience. In the end systematicity and extensiveness are judged by ourselves, and we might find that there is no *material possibility* of any increase of system. That would be independent of the logical possibility that for any degree of integration there might be a further degree, but that is not what is relevant to Kant's claim.

13 It may be that it is regulative for investigation, but constitutive of fact. 'Experience' is ambiguous between evidence and fact, and when Kant considered the matter with respect to the dynamical Principles, 'experience' was more like fact than intuition (evidence) (A180/B223). The passage at A650 makes it look constitutive. A647 talks of the employment of reason not being constitutive so much as heuristic.

14 As far as I know Kant nowhere uses the expression 'material possibility'. I am merely adopting his use of 'materially necessary', which is equivalent to strict universality, and using it for 'real possibility', actual at some time or other (as outlined in the Postulates). At B308 we are told the possibility of a thing can never be proved merely from the fact that its concept is not self-contradictory, but only through its being supported by some corresponding intuition.

15 Kant is insistent that the mere absence of contradiction in a concept is no proof of its real possibility (A244/B302, B308).

16 At A494/B523 Kant introduces the 'transcendental object' in quite a different sense from that which I suggested it has at A109. It would perhaps better be 'transcendent object'. Thus: 'We may, however, entitle the purely intelligible cause of appearances in general the transcendental object, but merely in order to have something corresponding to sensibility viewed as receptivity. To this transcendental object can be ascribed the whole extent and connection of our possible perceptions, and can say that it is given prior to all experience.' Without such an object appearances would not be appearances of something, and so indistinguishable from illusions. Thus, for example, A252: 'Unless we are to move constantly in a circle, the word 'appearance' must be recognized as already indicating a relation to something, the immediate representation of which is, indeed, sensible, but which, even apart from the constitution of our sensibility (upon which the form of our intuition is grounded), must be something in itself, that is, an object independent of sensibility.'

17 This is from a passage where Kant assimilates such things to 'noumena' understood in the negative sense, that is, to things in so far as they are *not objects of our sensible intuition*. In such a sense he is usually

thinking of things-in-themselves. But it also covers things that are objects of a receptive intuition other than ours, surely more phenomenal than noumenal, which tends to slip out of the picture. Again, that is distinct from 'noumena' in the positive sense, since those are thought of as objects of a non-sensible (non-receptive) intuition (B307), which is not what is in question.

18 Though he does appear to retract that in the footnote to B70, saying; 'The predicates of the appearance can be ascribed to the object itself, in relation to our sense, for instance, the red colour or the scent to the rose.' The aim is to avoid treating these properties as illusory, as Kant thinks we would be if we ascribed them to objects in themselves. Maybe he misses the intermediate position because he thinks that is claiming an unacceptably close grasp of the in-itself. In 1790, however, he uses the official idea again to argue that colours or tones could only be beautiful on account of their form. Their material quality cannot be assumed to be the same in all subjects (*Critique of Judgment* §14).

19 To the extent that Kant engages with that he seems to think that such intuition is not so much cognitive as creative (see B138–9, 161).

20 Their experienced world would undoubtedly need to register alterations and changes, and Kant is insistent that to introduce such concepts the idea of movement in space has to be drawn on (B291). It is difficult to see how that requirement could be represented as one that is restricted merely to our sort of intuition.

21 Just to put it in terms of possibility is very cautious. Others' experience must draw on the categories and the Principles no less than ours. The idea we are transcendentally committed to is of a unified system of nature under laws. Nature itself is for Kant the totality of all appearances, so not just appearances given to us in space and time, even though he occasionally expresses himself like that, but those given actually or potentially to others too. That, in turn, supposes a maximal systematization of nature that is not limited in the way that ours is bound to be.

Chapter 6: Cognitive Rewards

1 'Under the guidance of these principles, we discover a unity in the generic forms of the orbits, and thereby a unity in the cause of all the laws of planetary motion, namely gravitation. And we then extend out conquests still further, endeavouring to explain by the same principles all variations and seeming departures from these rules; finally, we even go on to make additions such as experience can never confirm, namely, to conceive, in accordance with the rules of affinity, hyperbolic paths of comets, in the course of which these bodies entirely leave our solar system, and passing from sun to sun, unite the most distant parts of the universe – a universe which, though for us unlimited, is throughout held together by one and the same moving force.'

2 We can even read the Refutation as a criticism of Descartes' famous would-be proof of his own existence in the *Second Meditation*. Descartes can only derive the conclusion that he exists from his thinking the proposition 'I am, I exist' on any particular occasion on the assumption that he can assert that at that time he is thinking that proposition, which of course presupposes exactly what he sets out to conclude. So, Kant will be saying that primary assumption cannot be secured from within the mind, as Descartes sought to do, but it does become available once we accept that perception gives us the external world directly. Only in that case, Descartes' proof of the self's existence loses its methodological interest.

3 The important work the understanding has to do for us to organize our world in space and time is insisted on at B160 fn.

4 The faculty of imagination is essential to the perception of objects in space. It has nothing to do with fantasy, which is what Kant is arguing against in this first Note.

5 Compare the clear consistency of saying of some competitive race: 'Each one of us may lose; but at least one of us must win.'

6 I am assuming here that, like his predecessors, Kant would not follow latter-day thinkers in taking knowledge to be a mental state. See in particular T. Williamson, *Knowledge and its Limits* (Oxford, 2003).

7 Curiously at A822/B850 Kant articulates a view of knowledge that is independent of truth, viz. the holding of a thing to be true which is both subjectively and objectively sufficient, subjective sufficiency being my own conviction and objective sufficiency that of everyone else. Rather cavalierly he remarks that 'there is no call to spend further time on the explanation of such easily understood terms'.

8 A third consideration on which Kant draws is the agreement of others, loosely prepared for in the Transcendental Deduction by the aspect of publicity that comes with 'relation to an object'. 'The touchstone whereby we decide whether our holding a thing to be true is conviction or mere persuasion is therefore external, namely, the possibility of communicating it and finding it to be valid for all human reason. For there is then at least a presumption that the ground of the agreement of all judgments with each other, notwithstanding the different character of the individuals, rests upon the common ground, namely upon the object, and that it is for this reason that they are all in agreement with the object – the truth of the judgment being thereby proved' (A820–1/B848–9).

9 'If we take away from our inner intuition the peculiar condition of our sensibility, the concept of time likewise vanishes; it does not inhere in the objects, but merely in the subject which intuits them' (A37). Also, 'It is therefore, solely from the human standpoint that we can speak of space, of extended things etc. If we depart from the subjective condition under which alone we can have outer intuition, namely, liability to be affected

by objects, the representation of space stands for nothing whatsoever' (A26/B42).

10 *Sixth Meditation ad finem*: 'the exaggerated doubts of the last few days should be dismissed as laughable. This applies especially to the principal reason for doubt, namely my inability to distinguish between being awake and being asleep' (Cottingham et al., eds, vol. II, p. 61).

11 Recall that the Second Analogy provides metaphysical underpinning for Newton's first law, the law of inertia, and it is only a loose application of that to say that things will persist unless something acts on them to bring about alteration. The understanding could not organize the world of appearance accordingly and yet leave Locke's worry still in place.

12 While the conclusions of sound inferences may not be confirmed by direct observation, this does not mean they cannot be confirmed. Given Kantian holism, observations of other things (such as laboratory equipment) will confirm inferential hypotheses when theory is well enough advanced, and well-established theory provides sufficient support for predictive claims.

13 These inferences will anyway only be to what Kant calls 'indeterminate'. They provide no specific knowledge about the in-itself, but just that something or other with its own internal character must underlie or ground appearances. For this, see B307.

14 This would be a particular instance of the two-world model of phenomena and noumena that appears at A249. But in the B version, that has generally disappeared in favour of two ways of regarding the same thing. We should think through the appearance of the self to inner sense (in one's own case) and outer sense (in the case of others, both they to us and we to them) in the same light, even if Kant does not offer much encouragement to us to do so.

15 And notice B415, quoted below as an explicit example to the contrary.

16 'Moreover, it must be acknowledged that perception and everything that depends upon it is inexplicable on mechanical principles, that is to say, by means of shapes and motions. And if we suppose there to be a machine, so constructed as to think, feel and to perceive, we could imagined it as enlarged while keeping the same proportions so that one might go into it as into a mill. That being so, we should, on exploring its interior, only find parts working one upon another, and never anything by which to explain a perception. So, it is in simple substances, and not in compounds or in machines, that perception must be located.'

17 *Nota bene*, there is no implication that in such a situation I think your thoughts any more than earlier the observant dentist was liable to suffer your toothache.

18 It is always illuminating to think of 'phenomena' and 'noumena' as nominalizations of the adjectival terms 'phenomenal' and 'noumenal'.

In that way the temptation to think of them as designating distinct entities is removed.

19 It is interesting to recall that precisely at this point Berkeley scoffs at the introduction of material bodies and says that a far more plausible explanation of our passivity is given by appeal to God and His inscrutable will (*Principles of Human Knowledge*, especially §72, but also §§26, 29, 57).

Chapter 7: Appreciation

1 Berkeley does in fact make the distinction by reference to considerations of systematicity. Since these are at the heart of Kant's own thought about truth and objective validity, Berkeley would have every right to feel aggrieved at Kant's dismissal of his views on this ground.

2 A project pursued in the *Metaphysical Foundations of Natural Science* (1786).

3 Kant's protest at the suggestion is to be found at A91–2/B123–4. Experience could not reveal the strict universality (i.e. necessity) that is internal to these concepts, most notably that of causation. As one might expect, the text reveals Kant locating the shortfall in the 'empirical' concept as due to the inevitable limitations of the abstractionist procedure of concept-formation he presumes it would have to rely on.

4 Kant himself explicitly resists all appeal to the identity of indiscernibles here, distinguishing similar appearances by their possessing different locations (A264/B320, A272/B328). At the present juncture, where identity of location is itself in question, congruent manifolds would be still distinguished independently of their being assigned a time and place by their different relations to distinct subjects.

A Very Short Bibliography

This orientation to the *Critique* has avoided all engagement with the enormous volume of secondary literature that has built up around it. Anyone wanting to pursue the various topics I have touched on, as well as those I have left alone, and to find alternative readings of Kant's text to what I have offered will find much of interest in the books listed below. Nothing, however, can be as rewarding as close attention given to Kant's own text.

Texts by Kant

Kritik der reinen Vernunft (1781, 1787), ed. R. Schmidt. Hamburg: Felix Meyner Verlag, 1956.
Prolegomena zu einer jeden künftigen Metaphysik (1783).
Metaphysische Anfangsgründe der Naturwissenschaften (1786).
Critique of Pure Reason, tr. N. Kemp Smith. London: Macmillan, 1929.
Critique of Pure Reason, eds and trs P. Guyer and A. Wood. Cambridge: Cambridge University Press, 1998.
Prolegomena to any Future Metaphysics as a Science, tr. and ed. P. G. Lucas. Manchester: Manchester University Press, 1953.
Metaphysical Foundations of Natural Science, tr. J. Ellington. Indianapolis, IN: Bobbs Merrill, 1970.

Kemp Smith's index to his translation of the *Critique* is an invaluable means of tracking down Kant's discussion of particular topics.

Secondary Literature

Allison, H. E., *Kant's Transcendental Idealism*. New Haven: Yale University Press, 1983.

Bennett, J., *Kant's Analytic*. Cambridge: Cambridge University Press, 1966.
Bennett, J., *Kant's Dialectic*. Cambridge: Cambridge University Press, 1974.
Bird, G., *Kant's Theory of Knowledge*. London: Routledge, 1962.
Brittan, G., *Kant's Theory of Science*. Princeton: Princeton University Press, 1978.
Dryer, D. P., *Kant's Solution for Verfication in Metaphysics*. London: Allen and Unwin, 1966.
Ewing, A. C., *A Short Commentary on Kant's Critique of Pure Reason*. London: Methuen, 1938
Friedman, M., *Kant and the Exact Sciences*. Cambridge, MA: Harvard University Press, 1992.
Gardner, S., *Kant and the Critique of Pure Reason*. London: Routledge, 1998.
Guyer, P., *Kant and the Claims of Knowledge*. Cambridge: Cambridge University Press, 1987.
Kemp Smith, N., *Commentary to Kant's Critique of Pure Reason*. London: Macmillan, 1923.
Körner, S., *Kant*. Harmondsworth: Penguin Books, 1955.
Langton, R., *Kantian Humility, Our Ignorance of Things in Themselves*. Oxford: Clarendon Press, 1998.
Paton, H. J., *Kant's Metaphysic of Experience*. London: Allen and Unwin, 1936.
Strawson, P. F., *The Bounds of Sense*. London: Methuen, 1966.
Walker, R., *Kant*. London: Routledge, 1999.
Walsh, W. H., *Kant's Criticism of Metaphysics*. Edinburgh: Edinburgh University Press, 1965.

Useful collections of articles:

Bird, G. (ed.), *A Companion to Kant*. Oxford: Blackwell (forthcoming).
Guyer, P. (ed.), *The Cambridge Companion to Kant*. Cambridge: Cambridge University Press, 1992.
Walker, R. (ed.), *Kant On Pure Reason*. Oxford: Oxford University Press, 1982.
Wolff R. P. (ed.), *Kant: A Collection of Critical Essays*. London: Macmillan, 1968.

Index